OUT OF THE WOODS

The Armchair Guide to Trees

Will Cohu

With illustrations by Mungo McCosh

 SHORT BOOKS

First published in 2007 by
Short Books
3A Exmouth House
Pine Street, London EC1R 0JH

10 9 8 7 6 5 4 3 2 1

Copyright ©
Will Cohu 2007

Illustrations copyright ©
Mungo McCosh

A CIP catalogue record for this book
is available from the British Library.

ISBN 978-1-904977-83-4
Printed in Italy by Graphicom

Contents

Foreword

*O*ut *of the Woods* is intended to fill a large gap in the tree bookshelf. Tree books tend to be divided along strict lines: detailed guides to foliage and sexual organs, quasi-religious texts about Wiccan practices and books featuring beautiful photographs of the authors posing by exotic trees in faraway places. All these can be very useful, intriguing and lovely to look at but none seem to help much when it comes to identifying a naked hedgerow tree or some miserable vandalised specimen in a supermarket car park in the depths of winter. In this respect, *Out of the Woods* will, I hope, be of practical help. On the other hand, you might just want to curl up by the fire and whizz through it in a couple of hours. That's what I would do, particularly if it was raining.

We can all agree that trees are wonderful and necessary things and most of us are probably just as unanimous in our ignorance about recognising them. Conventional tree guides are frustrating for the beginner: you have only to read the words "leaves pinnate" and the mind goes blank. This book is studiously non-technical. I have instead decided to take readers on a ramble around town and country, looking at the naked forms of trees, and imbuing them with whatever character makes sense to the casual eye. Trees, like birds, have an individual jizz which you can quickly pick up if you spend some time in their company. The secret is to look for yourself and to love what you look at. To this end I've included some biography and gossip about my subjects, and quizzes full of wholesome tree-jokes.

I have also taken the unusual step of focusing predominantly on trees in winter. For, as with the human body, the external form of a tree is shaped by its skeleton and thinking about the latter is a help to knowing the former. Naked trees are in many cases more articulate and interesting than are trees in their cabbage-like summer forms.

The book began with my determination to tell oak from sycamore as I drove along the motorway. This may sound curious but we all spend a depressing amount of time in the car and you might as well use it constructively. It is good to take an interest in the passing world: it makes you want to stop and take a closer look (though I should make it clear that I do not in any way condone drivers taking their eyes off the road other than to read appropriate information or matrix boards). I am now on nodding terms with some trees. Follow my simple techniques and you too could tell your sycamore from your oak at 70mph. (variable on the M25).

When writing about trees, it is important to get beyond the stage of crowning a new monarch every chapter. Nothing is more detrimental to pleasure for the reader than ever-increasing awe. Another occupational error of writing about trees – that goes back to the original tree-hugger, John Evelyn – is idealism, the love of a perfect form which in the case of that gentleman bordered on something almost pathological. It is in this tradition that most tree books include magnificent pictures of trees as you will never see them. I have never been that interested in valuing anything only for its size. Okay, so it is big: what else does it do?

This is a work of affection not horticultural scholarship. If something has looked like being a problem, I have gone around it. I have taken literary licence with names throughout, resisting the temptation to launch into fraught questions of taxonomy and nomenclature. None of this adds to the pleasure of looking at a tree. I have, for example, been very lax in making no distinction between Japanese cherries and Japanese flowering cherries, but to embark on Powell-esqe genealogy would leave no time for fun and, anyway, the taxonomists are always changing things. Inevitably, foliage is mentioned: many ornamental trees are hard to tell apart without flowers or leaves. But there are no complex descriptions and anyone wanting precise information can go to one of the recommended books at the back, where there is also an index of Latinate names. I have consulted widely but all errors are my own. Measurements are imperial – the metric ones never seem dramatic or precise enough. If I write six inches, you know what I mean, but if I write 15.24cm, you will have to reach for a ruler to find out that I meant six inches.

Disagreement about any of my descriptions is welcome, since the purpose of the book is to encourage readers to leave books behind and take their own imaginations out to play with the world.

My thanks to all at Rogers, Coleridge & White and Short Books, to Mungo McCosh for his lovely illustrations and especially to Kim and my family for their support.

This book is dedicated to Charlotte Brooks Cohu.

Will Cohu, May 2007

1. Glimpsed from a Car

You can spend years driving to and from work along the same stretch of dual carriageway without having a clue where you are. You are simply on the road and why be familiar with more than is necessary? The road requires most of your attention, shared as it is with many others lost in their daydreams and telephone conversations, all sleepily contriving to miss each other as they slip from one lane to another. The road takes you out of time. When you are on it, you are neither here nor there, but in motion, travelling along a corridor lined with trees that screen the world beyond. There are various entrances and exits along the corridor: a tired-looking garage at which you rarely stop because it is hell to pull back onto the dual carriageway; some boarding kennels located in a curious half-timbered villa and a long lay-by generally crowded with lorries. In summer the walls of the corridor are green. In spring they are splashed with white, in autumn red and yellow. This is what you notice as you pass at 70 miles an hour.

It is only when an accident or roadwork brings the traffic to an enforced, bored crawl that you look more closely at your surroundings. Let us suppose that such a crawl occurs on a day late in the year, one of those autumn days of poignant clarity when the weather is misty at the bottom and sparkling blue at the top. The leaves have turned and are dripping gold onto the roadside. Suddenly there are holes in the walls of the corridor through which you can catch a glimpse of a world beyond. Stuck in traffic, you stare at the naked trees and then you see through them, to the converging lines of a ploughed field, the mound of a distant hill, the tower of a far-off church and huge gateposts that frame an entrance to old parkland. Blurred with frayed mist and low sun, the landscape looks both mysterious and close, a profoundly beguiling, nostalgic illusion that you feel you could reach out and touch from the open window of your car.

Now, in late autumn, you notice the individual forms of trees which have emerged from the anonymous mass of summer growth. They are not all the same sort of tree. There are tall ones, fat ones, bristling ones, trees with branches like fat snakes or splayed forks, twisted small trees planted up embankments that you know are laden with blossom in the spring and gaunt monsters glimpsed in distant fields. These are the trees that have sheltered you and watched over you, swallowed your fumes and stopped you blowing off the road, year in and year out.

And yet you do not know their names.

Why should you care? Perhaps because it is rude not to know the name of something that works so hard on your behalf, or perhaps because of a feeling that the trees stand at the gateway to the horizon: they are guardians of the landscape and it may be that a quest for familiarity with them will provide you with a key to what lies beyond, a licence to walk and wander in the Elysian vision outside the corridor. Days such as this are precious and few and yes, it would be nice for once to stop driving to and fro and get out and walk. Just to take a breath of this air and look around. Why don't you bunk off work and we could go for a walk and look at trees? As for their names, you would be surprised at what you know, if you use your eyes. Yes, I hear you complain, that's all very well but you need leaves to identify trees and it is nearly winter now. Well, actually no. It can be more exciting looking at naked trees. They have a lot of character. And in their characters lie clues to their identity.

The traffic coughs into life and lurches forward. The landscape simmers in the mist as you crawl level with the lay-by: this is your last chance to stop. So, why not? Do it. Pull over.

The first thing you notice about the lay-by is the large pothole the car crashes down into. The hole marks a temporal boundary. In pulling off the dual carriageway you have gone back in time 30 years. This lay-by is a fragment of Britain unchanged since the 1970s, an ox-bow lake cut off when the road was straightened. Its surfaces are ravaged with water-filled ruts big enough for ducks to sail on. There are no public lavatories and its boundaries are marked by the spoor of travellers. Plastic bags and old newspapers hang in the trees and the far hedge line bulges with builders' wreckage and bin-liners filled with sinister lumps. There is a café run from a caravan that flies the Union Jack as if it is a distant outpost of Empire. It is popular with lorry drivers as a good kipping spot and is a well-known rendezvous for people in company cars, both for business and pleasure. The lay-by seems quite self-contained. It is ruled over by the man who runs the café. He probably issues a local currency and authorises elections.

As we step out of the car – mind out for the puddle – we make our first thrilling discovery. Look at the peculiar trees that line the ditch of the lay-by. Tall, slender trees with small black things hanging from their branches, trees that look from a distance as if they were small electricity pylons with those little ceramic fixtures through which the power lines run. But these fixtures dangle and, at a distance, it is not clear what they are, just some sort of dangly wotsit. The trees have no leaves, so they must be deciduous, and yet the shape of the wotsits is reminiscent of

Alder: a tree of slow-moving waters now stuck in the lay-by with its feet in a stream of effluent

cones that we know belong to pines, which are evergreen, of course. Come closer and you will see that the dangly wotsits are not one thing, but a mixture of bite-sized cones and little catkins. Two sorts of dangly wotsits! How exciting. Within five minutes of beginning this quest we have discovered something no one has ever seen before growing wild in a lay-by. Cones *and* catkins! This is surely a completely new species, some mutant grown wild among radioactive sludge dumped here back in the bad old days. You feel as if the lorry drivers and company reps queuing at the café for their bacon sandwiches have turned to look at you quizzically. Are you a spy? A council official? Someone come to threaten their fiefdom? They relax as they see your obvious pleasure in their trees. No problems. Just another tourist in their island paradise, looking at their alders.

The common alder is a thirsty tree that once grew thickly beside the slow-moving waters of southern England's narrow rivers. If you saw alders, a river was nearby. Alder wood was used in boats and jetties and underwater piles, and in the clogs worn by Lancastrian mill-girls. Families of "Cloggers" would buy up an acre or two of alders down along a river and move in under canvas to harvest the trees.

Now it is planted in the places we drive past – ditches, landfill sites, shelter belts and reclamation projects. It is more indicative of a river of effluent than one of water. It fixes nitrogen into the soil and prepares poor ground for other trees to follow, so there is something of the obliging engineer about the tree.

Thin and sparse when young, it develops into a glossy green spreading adult, with leaves square-tipped like a tennis racquet. The cone-like dangly wotsits are "pseudo-cones" first green, later brown, which develop from female catkins. The male catkins stay hanging in small, dull purple clusters throughout the winter and liven up by turning yellow in early spring.

Aha, but proud as the bacon-sandwich mob may be of their common English alders, the ones in their little-England lay-by are in fact foreign interlopers. They are Italian alders, an Armani version of the tree, distinctively conical when young and staying slender when older, with a sinewy black trunk that leans louchely. Their leaves are heart-shaped and glossy and fluttery and might be mistaken for the leaves of a lime or a pear. An Italian alder is most definitely a tree with airs and graces; it fidgets and twinkles among the rubbish and has bigger, sexier, danglier wotsits – larger cones and catkins. It grows fast and does not require the constant presence of water and so is now often used on bleak roadsides in preference to the common alder. It also likes the city – it is an Italian – doesn't mind the traffic and laps up the smoke. Being tall and slim, it adds shiny class to narrow streets in inner city boroughs and you can even see it dawdling around Mayfair, leaning out and nodding its catkins at the passing girls.

There are several other trees with winter or early spring catkins, some of which may be lurking in this lay-by. Birch for one, which you must admit is scarcely a hard tree to distinguish. It is a slim-waisted tree with delicate, coppery branches and a pallid, silver trunk. It is the ubiquitous background to Russian novels. How did it come to be here? If it wasn't planted, it may have come uninvited, arriving in a cloud of dust-like seed, fine as a puff of smoke.

Birches marched across the British countryside after the glaciers first retreated, and the tree is always quick to recolonise, given the chance, bursting out in patches as if the silvery nacreous residue of the past had suddenly overflowed into the present day. It never seems to grow in the right place and is constantly being cleared from one site while it is being planted elsewhere. Lay-bys and waste ground are weak points in time where plants from one age can slip through into the modern world and live for a while untroubled. Birch is one of these time-travellers, always lost, always at home, always planted, always unwanted, and travelling, always travelling. The sorrowful, weeping aspect of the silver birch seems to reflect this plight, but the birches in this lay-by look more upright and perky: they may be the more optimistic white or downy birch.

Hazel is another time-traveller from that ancient, cold climate, and there is plenty of it in this lay-by. Again, some of it must be here by design. Why is it that amenity planting schemes look so often and fondly back to the post-ice-age landscape? Are lay-bys and picnic areas designed to attract woolly mammoths? Or are they intended as environments in which only Yorkie-bar-eating Neanderthals can survive?

Hazel is a charming procrastinator that can't decide quite what it is. "Am I a tree or a bush?" it asks of onlookers. "Tree or bush? What do you think?" It has upright stems that are straight and glossy as walking sticks in an old umbrella stand and there are also crooked leafy branches that zig-zag quizzically, as if a plant pot had been dropped in the umbrella stand as well. Do not be fooled by its slenderness or its vagueness: hazel is tough and pliable and has been used down the centuries for weaving walls and fences.

In early winter fawn-coloured hazel catkins (those "lamb's-tails" of childhood) appear on spindly twigs. The leaves are big and floppy like some withered faddish vegetable. In late summer you might be lucky enough to find a few nuts if you can beat the squirrels to them. Perhaps some of those couples who meet here in their company cars present each other with ripe, soot-stained hazel nuts, the symbols of a perfect heart. There is something about those nuts. It is a very great mistake to plant a hazel in your garden if you have a possessive character. It is a grey squirrel issue. The thought of the grey tree-rat stealing their nuts drives people to the edge.

Though shrubby and anonymous in the winter, pussy or goat willow flourishes in the ditches here alongside the alders. It also has catkins in early spring, furry grey and silver for the girls, golden yellow for the boys. (The male catkins were used to decorate churches on Palm Sunday and were called "golden palms".) Our roadsides and riversides are thick with willows. Everybody knows the weeping willow so often planted by the tonsured edge of a village pond but wild willows are the prolific, overlooked beauties of the English countryside. Some make huge untidy trees that turn into hypnotically billowing clouds in summer, synonymous with lazy warmth and threatening collapse with every puff of a warm breeze. Some, like pussy willow or white willow, have blue-grey or pale silver leaves. Some produce coloured new growth, from yellow through to coral red. The bark colours are most vivid in late winter and stand out when viewed from the elevation of a passing train. Then you can see how the thick, leaning stumps of old pollarded (heavily top-cut) willows, shock-headed with red and yellow twigs, trudge along the straggling course of dykes and slow rivers. The willow

Do you know this leaf?

See page 254

takes a low, wet road and marks out an older, meandering countryside once travelled by Kenneth Grahame's Ratty and Moley and the gnomes of BB's *The Little Grey Men*.

It even moves itself by water. Crack willow, often a shattered sprawling monster falling into a river like a drunk in the last stages of summer heatstroke, sheds huge branches that float downstream and root themselves. In fact, willows are known for rooting from branches: having puzzled over a neat row of smashed old willows in Herefordshire recently, I realised that they must have started life as willow-wood fence posts. Now they are hollowed out and playing host to a burgeoning hedge of young hazels and hawthorns that, cuckoo-like, have found a home inside the old willow bodies.

There are other trees in this lay-by. Things with dark wood and thorns, things with brown dead leaves or dangling bunches of seeds like jailers' keys. There are red berries and withered yellow apples. But there are also those uncertain lumps in plastic bags and a strong smell of ammonia – the smell of a dead something – overlaid with the meaty waft of rose-pink bacon sarnies. It is always a good idea to get into the countryside around any foreign city. Behind the alders there is a stile and a sign – as strange under these circumstances as finding a doorway at the back of a wardrobe – which says "public footpath". Beyond, across the brown fields, under a shining sky is a hill crowned with a long, rounded, clump of trees. The wind is in our faces, the smell of bacon sandwiches is left behind. Shall we head off to the woods? You know you want to.

Bare essentials

COMMON ALDER – Upright spire when young but fills out. Conspicuous cones and pink catkins in late winter. **Leaves like tennis racquets**.

ITALIAN ALDER – **Armani version.** Spire when young, stays tall and slender when older. **Trunk bends elegantly.** Bigger cones and catkins. Heart-shaped leaves.

HAZEL – Umbrella stand with **escaping pot plant** in it. Fawn catkins in winter. Floppy large leaves like wilted vegetable. Nuts, if you can keep them.

PUSSY WILLOW – Large bush or small tree. Catkins are pussies in early spring on naked twigs. Silver pussies are female flowers: golden ones are male. Often in straggling self-seeded colonies along roadsides.

BIRCH – Silver birch weeps about its plight. Downy birch just gets on with it.

2. Into the Woods

Beyond the stile, the promised footpath has disappeared under the plough, but no matter. The sign points across a field that climbs slowly up to the little wood – the same spot on which the furrows of the plough seem to converge as if leading us to one objective only.

To the woods! How exciting to know that, just beyond the immediate world of tarmac and road signs, there is another, romantic, woodland world. There are hundreds of accessible little woods within a few miles of the biggest cities – visited infrequently, the destination of a Sunday afternoon march, but otherwise rarely examined. We like the woods, and know trees are a good thing. The woods are a refuge for merry outlaws, and trees are the beneficent playfellows of children, rich in mystic wisdom and thronged with fairies. But woods are not always benign and somehow they are all the more alluring for their dangers. The wolf waits for Red Riding Hood in the woods, and trees have eyes and there is that familiar phrase we know from the news: "The body was found in woodland…" A trip into the woods always has the promise of some intriguing discovery.

Let us trudge across the ploughed mud. I am sorry your footwear is inadequate. And your trouser bottoms are looking a bit dirty too. Funny how the wood is further than it first seems: it takes a small age for the noise of cars to recede but at last the drum of crawling engines is drowned beneath the cawing of rooks circling above the trees. Both of us are probably panting more than our vanity appreciates, but I promise you it will be worth it.

We are standing before a denuded wood. An overnight wind has completely stripped the trees. The ground is awash with long, thin green leaves, fat leaves with serrated edges, bright yellow ovals and splayed leathery hand-shapes. The trees are immense in their nakedness, rising and tangling, spreading and competing. Some of these trees are vast: your neck cracks as you gawp upwards.

So, how do you tell these trees apart without their leaves? Why not ask the wood? In fact, look: one monster at the edge of the wood seems to bend down to listen to you. The twigs that dangle from the pendulous branches are hooked and tipped with black buds as if it were giving you the come-hither with a crooked finger ending in a filthy, unwashed nail. I tell you, this tree has taken a fancy to you. It is big, but not altogether noble. Its trunk grows straight and thick to twice your height and then divides into limbs that soar skywards where a skeletal head is filled with the dark clutter of rooks' nests and clusters of brown seeds. If you cannot recognise those swaggering pendant boughs or the black buds, then the seeds are a give-away. Little seeds like the dried wings of beetles. In winter the blotches of seeds in the otherwise empty canopy are an unmistakable mark of an ash. No other tree of our countryside hangs onto its seeds in such profusion, as if it wanted them to jolly up its winter appearance.

Opinions are divided about the looks of the ash. The Rev William Gilpin, Victorian champion of the picturesque, remarked that "the ash never contracts the least disgusting formality" – meaning that it was regally arbitrary and romantic in its wild appearance. More recently, the late, great dendrologist, Alan Mitchell, took a different view: "The common ash has somehow become a byword in country literature and among poets for grace and elegance although in my view it is an exceptionally coarse and dull tree." Mitchell knew more about the height and girth of our trees than many before or since and he liked a good, thick, straight trunk he could get his arms around, but the ash was "much forked and graceless".

Certainly, its structure is never conventionally pretty: it is disrupted by schemes and diversions, by limbs that distract it and divide again into a sprawl of branches. It seems to be a character of minimal persistence in the straight and narrow. Those pendant boughs arise as a consequence of the ash shooting from the underside of an old branch, as if it had lost interest in growing laterally and fancied doodling with its own form.

The ash has Roman and Norse associations with divine authority which have conferred on it regal status, a king even among the many kings and queens of the tree world, which seems heavy with monarchy, like the latter stages of a dull chess game or some antique history primer. If the oak is king of the forest, the beech is queen of the woods, the sycamore is pretender to the throne, and the ash lords over the lot.

In order to know your trees you have to progress past blind reverence. Trees are simply large, woody plants that belong to the world of 120 million years ago. In that super-warm and lush climate, rich in carbon dioxide, they were the shrubs of the super-continents Luarasia and Gondwanaland. They stayed the same while the rest of the world just got smaller, and we are stuck in their undergrowth, looking up in envy. We stand in proportion to the tree much as the slug to the lettuce.

If the ash were to be a king, then it would be a slovenly, Georgian sort of king, a slut of a king, cunning, sexually ambivalent and instinctually promiscuous. It ought to grow tall and straight in solemn groves of cathedral proportions, but you will more often find it rolling drunkenly in your gutter, a skew-whiff sapling slurping a trickle of rainwater and dead leaves, or rising with silvery-grey grace out of a hole in your pointing. This monarch has never forgotten that the survival of a dynasty depends on the energy that took it from the street to the palace. Some of its character is written on the bark, which is an impressive piece of lattice work overlaid with a grey-blue fungal film, a marvellous heraldic design, but indifferently maintained.

Ash trees are lazy; they don't get out of bed till late in the year. When most other trees are busy doing wholesome spring things, the ash will yawn, turn in its bed, curl up its filthy fingernails and continue to dream of its excesses of the previous autumn, those wild nights swaying in the November winds. It loves winter. On stormy nights, the ash trees sway to and fro like mad old bastards dancing in the nude, their massive limbs wiping the clouds from the moon. Sometimes they do one hula too many, go pop and crack in two, just where a dose of the old rot has finally got them.

Provoked by the warmth of the spring sun, the ash tree's libido eventually stirs, and well in advance of its foliage it will push out flowers, like little tufts of purple broccoli on the bare twigs. Within its purple haze, still half asleep, the ash is busily fornicating, probably with itself. Ash trees can be male, female or both: they can change gender from year to year or have flowers of different sexes on the same branch. They are transsexual hermaphrodites. How convenient. This bisexual-transsexual-hermaphrodite creature wakes up late, pokes out a few flowers, plays with itself in the breeze, gets pollinated and goes back to sleep.

Some years it can't be bothered to produce any progeny at all, but when it has a good year, the seeds hang in bunches that crack thick limbs. Nonetheless, because it comes into leaf later than other trees, there is more light under its canopy in spring; and ash woodland can be rich in flowers. It is a model for higher authority, an ideal of the hands-off ruler, more interested in pursuing its own pleasures than in interfering with the lives of its subjects. It should be a Conservative ideal. The young foliage is rather pretty, coming out as epaulettes of bronze leaves that turn green later.

For many centuries the ash, not the oak, was the predominant woodland resource in Britain. Ash wood used to be harvested by coppicing mature trees – by cutting them down as close to ground level as a two-man cross saw would allow. The stump would then regenerate with several new shoots which could be harvested again from seven years onwards. Each time, the stool of the tree – that regenerating stump – would swell. In old ash woods that were coppiced you can often see these vast ancient stools, partly rotting. Several generations of a single family might have lived off the same few trees.

The mineral-rich foliage of the ash makes excellent fodder for animals (though in excess it can cause lethargy

An ash will make itself at home in your pointing.

known as "wood evil"); and its pale, elastic wood is as useful for tool handles and knife-blocks as it once was for spears and arrows. During the First World War, many fine ash trees were stripped out, as their wood proved invaluable for pick-axes, shovels and mattocks: some of those trenches that criss-crossed the Western Front must have been dug with ash that had its origins in the quiet midland shires of England. These days ash planking for kitchens is fashionable. However, finding ash suitable for modern commercial use is tricky: you need a tall stump, and ash is reluctant to do anything quite so dull as grow straight.

True beauty is never tidy, and ash is a tree of enormous character and in numbers it is a sure sign of good fertile land (to grow best it needs rich, damp but well-drained land). In Norse mythology, the tree of existence, Yggdrasil, was an ash. Man was formed from its wood. Its roots spread deep into the kingdom of death, while its boughs stretched outwards through time and space and contained the messy remnants of all that had happened. From its roots flowed streams containing knowledge of past and future events.

Ash trees were supposed to heal and I have read that in the late nineteenth century, sick children were still being "cured" by passage through a split in an ash. It also had a use in treating diseases of cattle which were supposed to have been caused by the malign activities of the common shrew. A live shrew would be buried in a hole in a branch of the ash which could then be applied to the afflicted cattle. Trees so used were called "shrew ashes".

There are many sorts of foreign ash trees and cultivars, most likely to be encountered in a park or arboretum. You may have weeping ash, white ash, green ash, Caucasian ash, Arizona ash, Texas ash, pumpkin ash, Manchurian ash, black ash and blue ash. The manna ash is a seductive tree: in spring it looks like it has been sprayed with gobbets of candyfloss, trailing great fluffy pony tails of sickly-sweet cream flowers. The Chinese flowering ash makes a nice small garden tree but common ash does not belong in close proximity to houses.

One of the themes of this walk will be how rarely we see trees in the ideal forms in which they are most often displayed in guide books. Here, in this wood, the giants are interspersed with stumpy trees and spindly trees, broken trees and doomed saplings. Some of these are small trees – hawthorns, blackthorns, hazel and field maples, of which we will have plenty later. But many are the runts of the big species, the stunted progeny of the so-called monarchs.

Is there an oak here? You would love to find an oak. And you are pretty sure you would know one if you saw one. Rising up among all the small stuff, there is something in its height, its thickness and the size of its naked crown that shows it must be an oak. Even without its leaves it has that rounded shape that children draw, and it has asserted itself among the tangle of other trees in a way an ash never could. Ash trees don't like being shaded out. They sulk.

But, if you think this tree is an oak, you are wrong. Look at the bark: oak bark is thickly ridged and brown while this bark is scabbing and coming off in grey and pink plates. It is a not an oak, but a sycamore, which has made quite a career out of being mistaken for something grander. Its Latin name is *Acer pseudoplatanus*, the false-plane tree, while its common name is said to record another confusion. "Sycamore" comes from *Ficus* (fig) and *Morus* (mulberry). According to Victorian sources – and they liked a good story – the tree was much planted in the fifteenth century by devout souls who mistook it for the species of fig mulberry Zacchaeus was said to have climbed in order to watch Christ's entry into Jerusalem.

The leathery, palm-shaped leaves superficially resemble those of the great London plane trees – even the bark, as planes also shed their bark in plates – and in the countryside the sycamore can look more like the idea of the oak than the oak itself, because one's idea of an oak is wrong. The characteristic of an oak is that it wants to grow widthways. Its lower limbs move out along the horizontal plane. The sycamore's limbs rise at 45 degrees, like upraised arms, and it has none of the great twisting internal engineering characteristic of an oak's structure.

The sycamore probably came from the mountains of central Europe hundreds of years ago. When exactly it arrived in Britain is a mystery but it is now thought of, perhaps harshly, as an unwelcome immigrant specialising in identity theft. Able to grow strongly even under shade, it hides behind other trees, playing the perfect shadow to their incomplete and partial forms, until it emerges suddenly as a dominant tree.

Accidental sycamores establish themselves so fast that they quickly assume the air of things planted intentionally. The average urbanite passing in and out of his subdivided house and mildly thrilled at the sight of any plant life among the broken motorcycles and upturned rubbish bins will assume a new sycamore sapling has always been there. Within a year or two it will have a preservation order slapped on it. It is all a matter of context, of course. In the right place a sycamore is one of the most useful and good-looking of trees and tougher than its rivals. You can see its energy in the stubby powerful fingers of its twigs, in its tumescent, bulging buds and the greedy little baby fists of its emerging leaves. It gives rapid shade for livestock and is immune to both city pollution and harsh weather. A mature solitary sycamore makes a compelling nude, an alert sentry watching over hedges or hillsides. In summer it has a comic vegetable vigour, like the silhouette of a giant cauliflower or a generous sprig of broccoli.

Purple and variegated sycamore cultivars are a vital part of urban planting schemes and some, for good or ill, are garden favourites. Sycamore wood is highly valued. It is pale and soft, does not taint food and is perfect for long-lasting kitchenware. Many of the fittings for the new Scottish Parliament were fashioned from sycamore, at huge expense. I have read that there was once an alternative public justice system associated with the tree – it was used as a gallows by the barons of the West and was known as the "doul" or grief tree, but this may be another bit of Victorian fancy.

If only the sycamore was prettier in summer: if only it had autumn colours. If only things could grow under it, then we might even like it. But we cannot forgive the horrible autumn leaves. They make a slippery mat underfoot that in cities inevitably conceals piles of dog-shit. The tree also has lots of basal growth – stiff shooting around the base of the trunk – which looks like unruly pubic hair.

We must hurry on into this wood if we are to find oaks. Fortunately, the winter sun is spilling through the open canopies of the trees. And, yes… there in a little glade are three oaks. You scarcely notice them at first, because they do not look like oaks are supposed to. They have gone lanky in the shade. Their trunks are slender, their bark is greenish and scarcely cracked into the long ridges characteristic of their kind; their limbs are small and high up.

But the parent of these oaks is not far away, on the other side of the wood. This is much more like it: an old tree, and a big one, now gone "stag-headed". A stag head of dead grey branches above still living foliage is not necessarily a sign of terminal decline. Sometimes, when the water supplies to the tree are cut, it will withdraw life from its upper branches. Trees surrounded by ploughed land will turn to stags if their roots are seriously damaged. Even the most withered oak can squeeze life out for another century.

The three smaller oaks here found their way into the wood 30 years ago, courtesy of a forgetful squirrel. The acorns were buried under an ash, dug out by a badger and trampled into the ground by children looking at bluebells. We can tell they are oaks because they have bristly, whiskery shoots coming out of what look like pigs' snouts, hither and thither up their trunks, and on these is the odd shrivelled oak leaf, the empty cup of an acorn and the round chocolate shape of an oak-apple. The whiskery shoots come from dormant buds in the bark – the tree's emergency rebuilding kit in case it is suddenly cropped. Sometimes the buds decide to wake up. Oak apples are those little fairy houses made by parasitic gall-wasps that children like to collect and store in jam jars and feed to their dolls or throw at each other. Children also love oak leaves, of course, green or dried. An oak leaf is the paw print of a large, amiable creature, it is a Christmas tree, a cheerfully deformed pear.

The naked form of a free-range mature oak is unmistakable. Its trunk is squat and thick, its lower branches grow sideways, while the rest of the tree is a matrix of massive serpentine limbs. In practice you rarely see an oak in its perfect form because it is so sprawling it requires perhaps a quarter of an acre to itself, about the same-sized plot as a generously proportioned family house. The canopy is so wide and low and level that the tree seems to hover above the ground like a freakish thunder cloud.

Among the virtues attributed to the oak is wisdom. It is a Buddha, a vast presence brooding over the perfection of its form for the 600 years or more of its lifespan. But if it is so clever, why does it grow so big? Think of those tons of wood it has to support, and not just outward growth, but those competing limbs inside its canopy. Surely a big tree must be more vulnerable than a compact one?

There are advantages to size. A big deciduous tree can compete more successfully for light and resources. A big tree can set more seed and increase its chances of having offspring. But to remain big and secure it must constantly adjust all its proportions. In their classic, *The Body Language of Trees*, Claus Mattheck and Helge Breloerin wrote: "A tree is a self optimising mechanical structure... such structures are as strong as necessary... an optimal structure has a uniform stress over the whole of its surface."

In other words, a successful big tree does not contain unnecessary timber. It is as economical in its construction as possible. It grows with a plan, trying to ensure that the

An oak wants to grow sideways; a sycamore raises its arms in benediction

physical stresses of its environment – wind, basically – are spread equally across its form. So a growing oak must add width as it puts on height, and given all the light it wants, an oak can be as wide as it is high. But if it is prevented from growing outwards, it will balance upward growth by adding wood to the branches inside its canopy.

A big oak is a safe tree because its wood is stronger. The wood has been subjected to massive stress from the weight of the limbs bearing down on it. When these limbs catch the wind and sway, they pull huge forces into the heart of the tree. In building its resistance to these, the oak creates the sinews that will keep it standing while centuries of concrete and steel rot away. It literally captures this elemental energy and locks it up. Hence, the strength of wood depends upon its experiences, upon the countless adjustments and compromises made to circumstance. Slender uprightness fits a tree for utility, not for longevity. It will make decent matchwood, but it will not support the roof of a cathedral.

Not all trees build for strength. Many have lightweight structures, like poplars, willows and birches. They make themselves as accommodating as possible to the wind and can expect a high mortality rate, although they produce many more seeds. A mature oak can drop 90,000 acorns in a season but the catkins on a birch will contain millions of seeds. Trees cannot actively plant their seeds. Each seed is either a hit or a miss, and so they compensate for a lack of mobility by increasing the probability of hits. Nature plays a numbers game, and the birch is better at it than the oak.

At first glance this is a conundrum. The oak is an architecturally inspiring structure. It is a living library, an important tree for bugs and birds (some 100 species favour it), rich in mythology and bound up with our sense of national identity. Its brilliantly engineered wood gives us one of the best construction materials. And yet, in this country at least, it seems pathetic at looking after its future.

The problem is the acorn. The oak puts a lot of work into those acorns. It may take half a century to pop its first crop. This living Buddha, this inscrutable meditating vegetable, perfecting itself while sheltering a catholic community of freeloading animals, has clearly thought long and hard about the message it can give the world. What sign might inspire the cruel and ignorant humans? Ah yes, the acorn: the world within a seed, the symbol of the connection between the smallest and the largest. Pick up an acorn and you possess the past and future within your palm. Perhaps half a millennium of growth is stored in this oval seed twice the size of a peanut. It is a miracle, this lesson in the significance of the slightest things. It is also very tasty to pigs, squirrels, mice, birds and insects and large enough so it cannot be missed by any of them. The vast majority of acorns are eaten. Most of the rest rot above ground.

Pollards and coppices

In traditional woodland management, wood was distinguished from timber. Wood was obtained by pollarding or coppicing trees, timber by felling trees completely.

Pollarding and coppicing are old ways of harvesting the wood from a tree. Both methods rely on the tree's ability to regenerate so that the wood can be cut at regular intervals. It is surprisingly hard to kill a healthy mature tree as it will always try to grow again using the energy stored in its roots, putting out new growth from buds stored within the bark.

Pollarding removes the upper limbs back to the principal trunk or bole. Coppicing cuts the tree down at the stump, leaving a stool. (Pollarding was most often performed where the new shoots might be vulnerable to grazing animals, as in hedgerows or parkland.)

In general, the growth produced by these methods would be "small wood", for fuel and estate work. Old woods and hedgerows are full of coppices and pollards. The techniques are rarely employed now. Trees in cities are pollarded either to restrict their canopies or reduce their need for root expansion, or just because they look striking.

If the oak survives without human intervention it is because it has struck a bargain with its predators. Squirrels or jays may take the acorns and hide them for eating later, but they often forget about them. Concealed in a bank or the bottom of a hedge away from the parent tree, one of the acorns may germinate and shoot up into clear space where it can grow without competition.

The tree is prepared to sacrifice 89,999 acorns to produce one perfect child. (In other European countries where there are higher rates of germination in oak forests, pigs or wild boar may play a part. They eat acorns, but they also trample them into the ground, in a similar way to what once happened in Britain's old forests where the swine were driven for "pannage".)

There are two principal varieties of oak in British woodland: the English oak or common oak or pendunculate oak, and the sessile oak. In theory, the sessile oak has a more upright shape, slightly different leaves and acorns that grow straight on the stalk. In practice, the two species can look similar.

Oaks vary greatly by locality – different bark, leaves, acorns, shape. However, sessile oaks were traditionally found in western Britain. Among the introduced species of oak are red oaks, scarlet oaks and evergreen Holm oaks. The red and scarlet ones come from North America. They have oversized leaves and roasting autumn colours, and grow very big, even for oaks. Holm oak is a tree with

Mediterranean origins that is often clipped and shaped in formal gardens.

Even today, there cannot be a sight more touching and pastoral than cows sheltering under the shade of an oak on a hot afternoon. But the history of the oak has not been peaceful: it is bound up with politics and war and money. Oak trees are at the heart of Britain's historic debate over land ownership. Whoever owned the oaks owned the people.

Storytellers put Robin Hood and his men in a hollow oak because it was a chance for the have-nots to reclaim what the rich had taken. From Tudor times through to the Napoleonic Wars, oaks furnished the Navy on which our military strength and trading wealth were based. "The tree of Freedom is the British oak," wrote Byron. Hearts of oak and all that.

British, or more specifically English-grown oak, with its spreading canopy, produced exceptionally massive twisted limbs, "crooked wood" or "compass timber" as it was known, which naturally formed the shapes needed for the basic skeletons of ships. There was no wood like it for strength, and for hundreds of years the supply of suitable naval oak was a recurrent anxiety to the state. From Henry VIII onwards, monarchs issued decrees circumscribing the use of privately owned oaks, often while raising cash by selling licences for indiscriminate felling in the royal forests. It was not just the Navy that wanted oak. Oak was the preferred building material for churches and houses. The ironmasters needed oak charcoal for smelting and the glassmakers for glass-blowing. The tanners wanted oak bark for tanning, dye-fixing and ink.

Not surprisingly, the history of oak woodlands has been the subject of furious debate. For many years historians assumed that these pressures destroyed all our best oaks and that the surviving trees were a pallid reminder of long-gone magnificence. In contrast, Oliver Rackham famously argued that the demands of industry had few long-term effects on our forests. Most of the oak used for smelting was taken not in the form of straight felled timber, but through coppicing or pollarding, which allowed woods to recover. But such is the persistently shrill note of anxiety in the historical records that there must have been a gen-uine fear of a shortage – if not of any old oak, then of crooked wood. For to build and maintain ships the trad-itional way took a lot of trees. In 1593, the Royal Navy used 1,740 mature oaks to repair just four ships. To build a new ship took 2,000 oaks, or 50 acres of trees. During Elizabeth I's reign a total of 34,220 tons of oak were cut for the Navy, or nearly 30,000 mature oak trees covering more than 800 acres of forest. It took at least a century to produce a suitable tree, so panic was understandable.

In time, new designs and techniques were tried. Straight oak was steamed into shape: some timber was imported and different trees used. But nothing did the job like twisted English oak. By the early nineteenth century crooked wood was worth its weight in gold.

In 1810, the great Gelynos Oak, outside Newport in Monmouthshire, was felled, carefully laid onto a bed cut from its own brushwood, and its timber sold to Plymouth Dockyard. Five men were employed for 20 days to cut the tree down and strip the bark and two men then worked six days a week for five months sawing it up. A century later the operation was recalled in the *Quarterly Journal of Forestry*: "The Main trunk was cut into quarter boards and Cooper's stuff; the Limbs, one upper piece stem for a one-hundred gun ship, one ditto 50 guns, one other piece 74 guns, three lower futtocks each one hundred guns, one fourth futtock one hundred guns, one ditto 74 guns, one ditto 44 guns, one floor timber 74 guns, one second futtock one hundred guns, and about 20 knees all of which were large enough for the Navy." The labour cost £82. The tree yielded six tons of bark, which fetched £200, and 2,426 cubic feet of timber, which went for £400. You can multiply these figures by 50 to reach modern values.

Naval timber had become an area of murky speculation. Shifty brokers controlled supplies, as increasingly the profitability of agriculture had made tree planting unviable for private landowners. Back in 1788 the Commissioners for Land Use had recommended that the state plant oaks for the Navy. But it was 20 years before the government at last did anything about it. Then the horticulturalist William

Billington was appointed by the Crown to superintend the planting of 11,000 acres of forest, predominantly oak "for future Navies" in the Forest of Dean, in those days a wet and hilly wilderness.

It was an arduous and heartbreaking process, all undertaken by manual labour. The nurseries had to be cleared and drained and fenced to exclude the sheep and cattle which roamed through the parts of the forest that were still common land. Billington's contractors put up 100 miles of stone walls and five-foot banks fronted by ditches and topped with thorns and gorse. They then planted hundreds of thousands of acorns and seedlings, which soon rotted from the wet or were killed by frost. At this, Billington developed a technique of raising seedling trees above wet ground by planting them in upside-down cut turfs. (Two hundred years later, when the Forestry Commission came to plant Kielder Forest in Cumbria, they encountered the same problems, and the same solutions had to be relearned all over again.)

In 1813 Billington realised to his horror that most of the trees were being eaten by mice. In one area of 1,700 acres, it was estimated that mice had destroyed 200,000 five-year-old oaks "besides the immense quantities from the acorns and seedlings". He ordered mousetraps to be dug, in pits 20 yards apart over 3,200 acres. In the winter of 1814 they caught 30,000 mice. Winters and springs back then were horribly wet and cold by modern standards, with heavy snow and harsh frosts. The soil was thin and the trees continued to fail and had to be replanted again and again. Billington, searching for clues to the constant set-backs, reckoned that the local fog must have poisoned the trees. None the less, through sheer persistence he improved the conditions sufficiently so that by 1818, there were more than four million oaks planted.

The oaks were to be trained to grow crooked wood, but they would never see action in a 74-gun ship. The land in the Forest of Dean produced poor timber and the oaks grew stunted and cramped. Anyway, by the time all this was apparent, the trees were already redundant. From 1840 onwards, iron replaced wood in shipbuilding. And before long, the repeal of the Navigation Act and the lifting of import duty meant that foreign timber could be imported cheaply, and goods no longer had to be carried in British-built merchant ships. The price of English oak began to fall. In 1862, the success of the "iron-clads" *Merrimac* and *Monitor* in the American Civil War brought the age of oak to a close.

A walk through some parts of the Forest of Dean is not a trip through a natural oak-wood landscape but a trip through an abandoned munitions factory, stocked with supplies for sea battles that were never fought. But then, much of what we romantically consider to be ancient and wild in our landscape owes its character to old working practices and long-abandoned speculation.

As for this little wood that we now stand in, it seems unlikely that it was a landowner's punt on a future conflict: its use was probably more domestic. Almost certainly it is a remainder of something larger. There are many thousands of woods like it all over Britain, small mixed stands of oak and ash and sycamore, that formerly supplied people with much of the fuel and building material and even animal fodder they needed. Now they live on, little visited or used, echoing in winter with the ghostly sound of the cross saw and axe.

Bare essentials

ASH – **Come-hither curled twigs** give look of descending even as it goes upwards. **Dirty black fingernail-buds.** Short bole. Erratic form. Generally the last to leaf up. Clutches of dried seeds in its canopy.

OAK – Huge sideways growth given space. **Massive engineering** within its canopy. Brown ridged bark. Golden new foliage. Cloud shape.

SYCAMORE – **Cauliflower shape**. Very busy around the edges. Branches ascending like upstretched arms. Sometimes flaking green or orange bark. Big tight buds. New foliage sometimes flushes purple.

Do trees *think?*

Trees have no brains and no physiology like animals but are able to create, maintain and adjust enormously complex structures. Quite how they do this is currently beyond human understanding: the mechanisms are so simple and yet interrelate so subtly. Human organs remain the same but increase in size all our lives: we are always big babies. A tree, on the other hand, increases by replication of its basic design.

The fundamental unit of a tree is a year's growth – a simple twig. And a huge tree builds itself by repeating the same pattern over and over again, adding more and more identical twigs. The pattern of the branches will imitate the pattern of the leaves. Thus trees with alternate leaves on their twigs – oak and beech – have alternate branches. Those with opposite leaves, like sycamores or maples, expand in a series of opposite branches.

There is no nerve centre in a tree – growth and shape are controlled by hormones secreted by the shoot tips, the roots and the leaves. Though these sources collaborate, there is also a hierarchy of control dominated by the lead shoot of a tree. This uses hormones to exercise "apical" control and suppress all lower growth of buds. The strength of regulation varies from total dictatorship to enlightened despot-ism and breaking the lead shoot off a tree will cause a revolution, an eruption of growth lower down as control is removed. Oaks, for example, have only moderate apical control, and have a sprawling shape. But control is strong in pines which are upright and narrow.

By manipulating hormones, trees are also able to respond to changing circumstances: they can sense prevailing winds and lay down "reaction" wood to thicken and reinforce exposed surfaces; they can adjust their direction of growth to compensate for injury; and shed branches that are problematic or suppress bud growth to create reserves. Defence is an expensive investment for a tree so it is used selectively. Hawthorns, for instance, will be at their thorniest up to six foot from the ground – the area where they are most at danger from grazing. And a hawthorn that has not been grazed or pruned for years may lose its thorns, although it will rejuvenate savagely when the tree is pruned or nibbled. Hollies are spiny at the bottom for the same reason. Yews have poisons in their foliage which have been found to be more concentrated when a tree is frequently trimmed – hence the more delightful and precise your topiary, the more toxic it will be.

3. The Slinky Beech & Her Drudge, the Larch

There are no beeches in this little wood of oak and ash and sycamore. Where is the beech? Surely in this supposed monarchy of the trees, the oak, ash and beech ought to co-exist? In fact, you will not always find them together because one tree does not necessarily enjoy the soil that pleases another. Most trees will flourish on any fertile soil, but their individual preferences are exaggerated because we use land to its best economic advantage. Woodlands are planted on less valuable land – dry land, wet land, high land. And if a particular tree is known to tolerate a particular environment it will be used as the primary planting and will become associated with that environment.

Thus, the chalky-white hills of the Cotswolds and Chilterns in southern England are known for their stands of beeches (called "hangers" from an Old English word "hangra" meaning "small wood") and are generally thought of as the natural home of beech, though many of the beeches were probably planted in the early nineteenth century. The trees were conveniently placed for the Thames Valley and High Wycombe, not so long ago the place where bent-wood chairs were made from English beech, beloved by English woodworm. But you could plant a beech in the soil of most gardens. It doesn't much like the clay on which oak and ash luxuriate, but it would probably survive.

To see beeches we should leave our little wood of oak and ash and follow the path gently upwards along a ridge. Up here the chalk and flint rises to the top of the soil and just below the crest, behind broken-down palings and twisted rabbit wire, is a plantation of beeches, growing in solemn, clean rows.

Beeches have their ardent admirers. Gilbert White, bachelor vicar of Selborne, thought the beech "the most lovely of all forest trees, whether we consider its smooth rind or bark, its glossy foliage or graceful, pendulous boughs". There is something feminine about the beech, or rather it embodies some unreformed notions of femininity. Men fawn over its sleekness and its well-toned skin, like randy Lilliputians staring up the legs of a giant woman. Cor, what a stunner! You can see this one looks after herself! Been giving those buns a work out! Look at those slender, muscular arms and those torpedo-like buds! And that full, blow-dried head of hair!

Should this be the standard of natural beauty? A tree that looks as if it has just emerged from a wax and massage, that slips quickly from main trunk into limb without any sign of a joint, as if coated in lycra? Where are the friendly knobs and bobs and burrs and descending boughs? Beeches do not welcome climbers. An ash will offer you a hand up, an oak will extend an arm down but the beech flashes a smooth length of leg.

This is a lads' mag tree, the catwalk creature of the woods, winsomely pretty in the spring with her diaphanous green leaves, crisply romantic in the autumn, dressed in red and gold for the party season. Even when a couple of hundred years old she looks like a million dollars. Okay, maybe she does a bit of botox, with that numb, nerveless look. But you've got to admire a woman who looks after her appearance. Plant me a beech. Plant me an avenue or a wood.

There is something too damn quiet about beech woods. Even this little beech plantation is a peculiarly silent, denuded place. Under the winter sun, the clean, spare, grey lines of the trees preside over long, empty avenues in which our voices sound muffled. There is nothing underfoot but leaf mould and the odd bramble. To some, beech woods are nature's cathedrals, but looking at the lines of identical trunks in this little plantation, it is like being behind bars or as if we had wandered into the landscape of *The Hobbit* and become lost in the fringes of Mirkwood, home to grouchy elves and giant spiders. Why is the wood so silent and lifeless and uniform? Why does the pretty beech makes such a sombre home for herself?

The beech has a special gift, not always evident when it is used as a roadside or parkland feature. Its branches are arranged in overlapping planes so that it casts a perfect blanket of shade. Little will grow under a beech. It was this power to generate darkness that gave the beech its secret life as the hired assassin of the forestry industry, a Nikita that smothers other trees to order.

By and large, the objective of forestry is to grow straight lengths of quality wood as quickly as possible. The valuable timber of a tree is all in the butt – *ie* the trunk, before it divides into branches. If trees put their energy into growing upwards, not sideways, then the butt can be lengthened. Trees are naturally light-seeking and can be bullied into growing upwards by shading their sides to kill lateral growth and to suppress the generation of under-growth. So, timber trees are often flanked by "nurse" trees that cast a dense shade. The trees most commonly used as nurses these days are evergreen pines, firs and cypress but traditionally some of the best "butts" of oak, ash and sycamore were cultivated alongside beeches.

This killer gift ensures that when the beech gets a foothold in a wood, it will, in time and through its wiles, come to dominate. Once beeches have a grip, they will shade out competition and establish their school of

monotonous perfection. Were it not for the saving intervention of the rabbit, which likes to nibble on a beech, the
whole country would fall under the sway of these evil
trees, which would march remorselessly from coast to
coast in lines of well-toned trunks, urging us to take up a
life of increased physical vigour.

My objections are prejudices against the obvious.
Privately, I sometimes enjoy ogling at a beech as much as
anyone and I particularly like the extremities of winter
beeches, where their twigs tail off smokily into the pallid
skies. When they are young or below about eight foot in
height, beeches may hold onto their leaves in winter – a
trait that occurs in other trees – and they whistle and rat-
tle in the wind. A thick beech hedge takes time to grow but
is the best of dens for children. I dislike the angry purple
of the copper beech – that symbol of municipal sophistica-
tion that dominates many parks – but could stare for hours
at the luscious, wet coppery reds of its first growth.
Legend has it that the copper beech is stained with blood
because it originated in Switzerland on the site of a double
murder. More likely it was found in Germany in the mid-
nineteenth century.

Sometimes the beech becomes intriguingly sculptural,
as if being candidly revealing about its secret character –
mostly when it has been pollarded or lopped for hedging
or has a few scars. Old hedge beeches may grow to
embrace adjacent fences, creating vignettes of startling

eroticism in which the skin of a tree appears to be pierced and pulled by barbed wire or the trunk suddenly gapes into a puckered mossy darkness where a fence post once was before it rotted away.

But if the beech is adept as squeezing out other trees, it also leaves them a lasting legacy. Plant beeches on poor chalk soil and in a couple of hundred years its potash-rich leaves and the fall of its beech mast – the tasty nuts popular with wildlife and pigs (even though they contain a mild toxin called fagin) – will produce decent enough topsoil to support many other species.

Up until the late-1960s beech wood was still in demand – not just for chairs, but for toys, high heels and the parquet flooring that was a feature of old schoolrooms. Like many others my school life was lined with beech wood, from the wobbly blocks of parquet flooring that could be kicked and rattled in boring lessons, to the soft, easily engraved desks and the click-clack heels of the teacher. These days beech is sometimes still used in plywood, in which form it went into the de Havilland Mosquito, one of the most graceful aircraft of the Second World War. But it does not weather well and it has little strength down the grain so is no use outside. Its softness makes it easily workable and in the past it was rough- shaped in the woods by "bodgers" before being sent on to the factory. It has always made good firewood: and it can still tout its looks and the withering stare of its shade.

This little beech wood is mainly playing nurse to rows of ash but the plantation also has blocks of larch, our only commonly planted deciduous conifer. At this time of the year the larch needles have turned a sour, smouldering yellow, a colour that dominates upland hillsides where there are large larch plantations.

Larch is a native of the Carpathian Mountains of eastern Europe and was imported four hundred years ago for ornamental planting. It did not at first impress. In 1791, Gilpin wrote that "it is little more than the puny inhabitant of a garden; or the embellishment of some trifling artificial scene". He had not seen a mature specimen which can reach 100 foot and makes a sweeping, cone-shape with pendulous branches and a nodding top like an old-fashioned sleeping cap.

Larch is the Cinderella of silviculture, a Carpathian drudge who does the hard work uncomplainingly. She makes useful timber and does all the nanny and nursing stuff cheaply and effectively, and given half a chance can steal the show. The tree looks miserable in winter, its needles like swags of melancholy old muslin. Very much Miss Haversham. But in spring it comes out to play with a fireworks display of happy growth, pushing out pale green needles in bunches of thirty, then male flowers as soft yel-

The beech, her branches trailing off smokily into the winter sky; and in the background the larch, her dutiful nurse

low finials and pink female flowers that form endearing, perfect mini-cones. The larch is perfect for cheerful demonstrations of basic biology to children – look, here are little yellow boy-flowers and here are pink girl-flowers, and they are the ones that will have babies! Yes!

Two hundred years ago, larch was being hailed as the new wonder-wood, the saviour of British forestry that promised an inexhaustible supply of quickly grown timber produced on otherwise unprofitable land. Its popularity was largely down to the Dukes of Atholl, who discovered that larch grew on mountains in Scotland, just as it grew on mountains in Europe. For three generations the dukes planted larches, higher and higher across their lands, where nothing else grew among the rocks. Between 1738 and 1826, they planted some fourteen million larch trees. The fashion for plastering mountains with conifers was set and the British landscape was changed forever.

In the mid-nineteenth century, the larch offered better returns than almost any tree in Britain. It could be cut when only three or four inches in diameter and used down the mines as pit props. The wood was big-hearted, strong and surprisingly tolerant of changes in temperature and humidity. It could be used in construction work and even for boat-building. It gave warning when it was stressed and bent and bulged rather than snapped suddenly.

Used as a dutiful nurse, larch was often planted alongside prized timber trees like Douglas fir. It could keep its neighbours clear of their side-branches for 25 years, until the big trees had "got away" tall and straight, and its deciduous needles made a dense, acidic mat that kept the weeds down. Beech and larch were considered good partners. The larch nursed the young beech and then could be harvested at 40 years old, while the beech could be grown on for another 40 years.

But larch is not immune to cold and it hates too much water. Like any tree, it prefers easy conditions to grow to its best size. As far as mountain planting went, it gradually came to be seen as perhaps not the most efficient of trees. As the economic pressure increased to use ever-higher and wetter land for tree planting so the hunt was on for even tougher species, and the most planted tree in Britain is now – by some margin – the Sitka spruce, a conifer from the coast of north-west America.

The larch used in commercial plantations these days is generally *Larix* x *eurolepsis*, a hybrid between European and Japanese larch which occurred naturally at Dunkeld in Scotland, where the Dukes of Atholl had planted both species, and which combines the fast-growing qualities of Japanese larch with European hardiness.

One side of this little plantation has been thickened against the wind by the addition of cover for shooting – a mixed bag of trees probably bought as a job lot out of the back of a garden centre, where the plants that have lost their labels are kept. There are all sorts here – even fruit trees – but also something that looks like a beech. It is a short, young, busy tree, its slender upswept branches forming a dense cocoon above its short bole; and it is holding onto its dead, oval leaves, just like a beech. But the grey trunk is lean and twisted and the buds do not stand proud from its twigs like the torpedoes of the beech – they are flush with the wood.

This is the hornbeam, a rough, tough little native. The confusion with the beech is historic – it is even known as horse-beech in some areas – and it probably ended up at the back of the garden centre because after losing its label, none of the staff could decide what it was. In summer it is even more easily confused with the beech because of the resemblance between the leaves. (The leaves of the hornbeam are coarse, and have hairs underneath, while beech leaves have soft gossamer hairs along their edges when they first emerge.)

The hornbeam is the tree that stayed down on the farm while its more glamorous twin took the limelight. Where the beech is curvaceous and well toned, the hornbeam is sinewy and muscular, as if it had spent its life digging ditches and breaking stones.

It is not tall and statuesque like the beech and its bark is often twisted and fluted so that the trunk looks as if it has been squashed flat. It can appear "fasciated" – composed of several stems growing together. Occasionally you might also see "inosculation" – the apparent union of branches that are growing separately further down the tree.

The wood of this little tree is exceptionally hard. The fluted or flattened bole is not a deformity of disease, but a sign of strength. For the wood of the hornbeam is shot through with exceptionally large medullary rays – the cells that piece together the annual rings of wood – so it is as if the tree has been transfixed with countless reinforcing bolts that have been tightened to the maximum and have altered the shape of the trunk.

Hornbeam was coppiced for poles that could be used inside or outside, while the timber made chopping blocks, shoe lasts, skittles, wooden screws, gun butts, industrial cogs and pulleys – anything that was required to take a real flogging. It burns slowly and so was also the ideal fuel for bakers' ovens.

Alan Mitchell dismissed the hornbeam as a "pleasant, if rather dull tree". Certainly, its beauty is nothing to do with size. The irregularity of hornbeams is fascinating. They remind me of the archers of the Middle Ages, whose skeletons were dragged from the wreck of the *Mary Rose* and found to have a twisted deformity of the spine from the immense force required to draw the old long bows. In the spring the tree has little green catkins while in autumn tassels of fruits hang like skeins of drying herbs from the it, as if these stocky blokes had popped on gorgeous earrings.

Hornbeam was once native south of a line between

Worcester and Norfolk, but modern shelter planting has made it ubiquitous along roadsides. It also makes superb hedging. There are various popular imported species and cultivars. The neat egg shape of the upright – "fastigiate" – hornbeam is a familiar sight in parks.

Around London, both Highgate Woods and Epping Forest are rich in old hornbeam coppice. On November 11, 1860, the hornbeams in Epping Forest were the site of an historic showdown. Thomas Willingale of Loughton went to the woods to lop hornbeam poles, as was the right of commoners of the parish. But the Crown, which had formerly guaranteed the commoners' rights, had recently sold its interest in the land to the adjacent Lords of the Manor, who had "enclosed" it. Willingale was arrested and jailed for two months. His case was taken up by the Commons' Preservation Society and then the Corporation of London, which had an interest in the forest. After a battle lasting 22 years, Epping Forest was saved as a public open space – a landmark in conservation.

The early management of Epping Forest was influenced by the pioneering conservationist Edward North Buxton, who, amongst much wisdom, expressed a dislike of pollarded trees. Buxton, said a contemporary, considered pollards were "not strictly speaking trees at all, but strange fantastic vegetable abortions... it is no more nature's idea of primeval woodland than are closely cropped hair and shaven lip and chin her intention for the real expression of the human face." Hence, forests that had been coppiced or pollarded for wood for hundreds of years were no longer cut or managed and the trees have regenerated rampantly into massive aerial thickets.

Our little plantation of beech, ash and larch looks forlorn and bereft. Will its wood ever be required? Who will come and cut it? Rabbits and squirrels have got in and have ripped away the bark at the bottom of the beeches, some of which already have horrible dark hollows of damaged and rotting wood. The skin of beeches is thin and they are vulnerable to attack for the first fifteen years of their lives. Chalky regions where beeches thrive are also the areas where in hard winters there is least forage for rabbits and so the trees are most likely to be chewed. Hornbeam is also attacked by rabbits, but it is tougher and can survive.

A few pheasants scurry away among yellowing larches. Time to get on. The path continues along the top of a low hill. There is evidence here and there of shooting, of game crops of maize planted in stands. There are isolated old farm buildings, and distant hedgerows with some large trees. Perhaps you can pick one or two of them out now: an oak with its sinewy, stocky growth and a large, lateral, low branch; the sycamore over there with its arms raised in benediction. The seedy ash trailing its fingers over an adjacent horse: nice rump.

Bare essentials

BEECH – **Aloof** tree, fit body, tight, smooth, grey bark. Slender torpedo buds standing proud of twigs. Early spring growth gives a purple hue to distant stands. Overlapping planes of branches give dense shade.

LARCH – Pagoda-shaped with sweeping branches. Yellow or orange in winter with dead needles and little cones. **Bright green in early spring** with pretty pink or red flowers. European version has nodding top: Japanese version has orange bark.

HORNBEAM – Small, stocky tree. **Fluted, twisted, muscular form**. Buds flush with twigs. Little catkins in early spring before leaves and dangling bunches of winged seeds in autumn.

Revision **quiz I**

1. **Which of these is characteristic of the oak?**
a) Black buds
b) Massive lateral limbs
c) Angry pixies

2. **An ash tree in winter**
a) Has bunches of brown seeds in its canopy
b) Skeins of drying acorns in its canopy
c) Holds onto its leaves

3. **A mature sycamore may have the shape of**
a) A lettuce
b) A cauliflower
c) A carrot

4. **Larch is**
a) Deciduous in winter
b) Deciduous in summer
c) Evergreen

5. **Common alder has**

a) Nuts and catkins
b) Clogs and catkins
c) Cones and catkins

6. **Crack and pussy are**
a) Two species of hornbeam
b) Two things that gladden the heart of a rapper
c) Two species of willow commonly found along roadsides and damp waste ground.

7. **Italian alders have leaves that are**
a) Hand-shaped
b) Heart-shaped
c) Liver-shaped

8. **Sycamore wood**
a) Does not taint food
b) Is highly elastic
c) Oxidises red when cut

9. **What is the most**

planted tree in Britain?
a) Oak
b) Sitka spruce
c) Copper beech

10. **The use of larch was pioneered by**
a) The Dukes of Atholl
b) Henry VIII
c) Robin Hood

11. **In forestry, beech has been useful to**
a) Restrict lateral growth on other trees
b) Restrict access to visitors
c) Restrict the presence of grey squirrels

12. **Which of these is a correct description?**
a) Beech buds are flush with the twigs: hornbeam buds stand proud
b) Beech buds stand proud of the twigs: hornbeam buds are flush

c) Hornbeam is a native of Norwich: beech of High Wycombe

13. **What is the difference between coppicing and pollarding?**
a) Coppiced trees are repeatedly harvested at the base: pollards have their upper limbs removed
b) Pollarded trees are harvested at the base: coppiced trees have their limbs removed
c) Coppiced trees have their bases removed leaving the pollards standing

14. **In Norse mythology, what sat at the top of the ash?**
a) An eagle
b) A squirrel
c) A chicken

15. **The term "crooked**

wood" describes
a) Epping Forest
b) The naturally bent oak limbs favoured by ship-builders
c) The limbs of sycamores on which Scottish outlaws were hanged

16. **Which of these can greatly control the growth of a tree?**
a) Mild summers
b) Hormones secreted by the lead shoot
c) Classical music

17. **Oak and ash like**
a) Chalk soil
b) Rich damp soils
c) Thin acidic soil

18. **Beech has**
a) Smooth, tight grey bark
b) Fasciated and inosculated limbs
c) Vigorous basal suckering

19. **A stag-headed oak**
a) Has antlers of new growth
b) Is used for mounting hunting trophies
c) Dies back at its extrem-ities often due to water loss

20. **Which of these is an accurate statement**
a) Oaks and beeches have alternate leaves and branch-es: sycamores and maples have opposite leaves and branches.
b) Oaks and sycamores have opposite leaves and branch-es: maples and beeches have alternate leaves and branches.
c) Sycamores rarely set viable seed

4. *The One-Stop Hedgerow Shop*

Our footpath now goes downhill until it joins a rough, pot-holed track that runs away towards tall trees that cluster around the domes of farm buildings. Beyond, the tower of a church stands silhouetted black against the afternoon sun. On one side the track is edged by a flailed, low hawthorn hedge. It is conscientiously neat, the work of one of those old boys who tell you that a hedge needs cutting twice a year to stop it "getting away". The other side of the track is different, perhaps because there is a whiff of a boundary dispute. Beyond a gate topped with admonitory notices sits a clutch of dilapidated buildings. The hedge on this side of the track has been left uncut so long that it has risen and thickened into a belt of trees, whose oft-decapitated forms have now sprouted a multitude of jostling new heads.

These hawthorns are wholly different from the trees only a few yards away, which have had their snaking stems and sharp thorns cut improbably into a neat square, so that all their energy seems furiously concentrated inwards.

They have escaped servitude to become craggy, with entwined silver and brown trunks like thick lianas, and branches streaming with barbed twigs heavy with berries of flat matt crimson. The hedge is splashed with this red: it is an inimitable and contradictory colour, dull but rich. It has blood in it and soot. It is a nursery colour seen in sales and antique shops, the colour of toy steam trains, lead-red aeroplanes and tin soldiers, the covers of old Christmas annuals and the posters of Technicolour films.

A hedge was once a rather nominal boundary made up of a great variety of sturdy shrubs or trees, a kind of natural market that could be raided for timber, firewood, animal fodder, fruit and nuts and even basic medication. The planting of purely hawthorn hedges is a relatively recent development dating back to the latter stages of the "enclosures". From the sixteenth century onwards the structure of rural Britain began to change as forest, heath and parcels of common land – used by the locals for grazing and foraging – were merged into private holdings and enclosed by hedges, walls and ditches. The process accelerated during the eighteenth and nineteenth centuries when the growth in population made agriculture necessary and profitable. By Parliamentary consent much uneconomic common land was sequestered by landowners. Fast-growing and hostile hedges were required to keep out trespassers and animals. Hawthorn was ideal: it grows rapidly into an impassable barrier – hence its old name of "quickthorn".

And soon some 200,000 miles of hawthorn hedges were planted.

The process of enclosure was often traumatic and even violent, though it certainly helped shape a lawless wilderness into the productive and idyllic chequerboard landscape that still characterises some areas of lowland Britain. It must have been galling for the commoners to see the hawthorn employed to keep them out of their former lands. For the hawthorn, or white thorn, was one of the small trees of woodland and waste that had a deep resonance for ordinary people. It was a bridge between the mundane and the supernatural. It was a haunted tree, a friend and protector, the outstanding beauty of the countryside when laden with blossom, and sometimes an ominous presence.

Even today there is in England a strong reluctance to bringing hawthorn blossom into the house, because death will follow. But this is not everywhere true – in parts of Ireland and Cornwall it seems to have been unlucky *not* to bring hawthorn into the house on May morning. Why should you not bring into your house the prettiest flower of the spring, those twigs clustered with blushing white, giving off that warm musky scent?

It is, admittedly, a complex smell, a bouquet of divergent and contradictory notes that not everybody appreciates. It is honey-and-almonds and dirty knickers. It is vivacious, seductive and, at the same time, like flesh that is on the cusp of rotting. It is a whiff of sex and death in the infancy of the year.

The hawthorn plays an important part in Proust's scheme of sense and memory. In *Swann's Way*, the first part of *A la recherche du temps perdu*, the taste of almonds in the famous Madeleine cake with which the novel begins, takes us back to an earlier memory, to the smell of almonds from hawthorn blossom and an intense religious and sexual awakening. Walking by Monsieur Swann's garden, the young narrator finds the whole path "throbbing with the fragrance of hawthorn-blossom. The hedge resembled a series of chapels, whose walls were no longer visible under the mountains of flowers that were heaped upon their altars." There were trees with "a thousand buds... swelling and opening, each disclosing as it burst, as at the bottom of a bowl of pink marble, its blood-red stain." Haplessly overwhelmed by obscure desires, Marcel stumbles across the young Gilberte and loses himself to an obsessive love that will have a bitter conclusion.

In fact, hawthorn does contain the authentic smell of death, which it exploits for sexual purposes. Hawthorn blossom secretes trimethylamine, a chemical found in the first stages of putrefaction in corpses. This attracts flies to the blossom, looking for carrion on which to feed and lay eggs. The rose-like flowers of hawthorn are "perfect" – that is, they contain both male and female sexual parts – and require only the movements of small insects to transfer pollen short distances. Flies do the job very efficiently. The admonition against bringing hawthorn blossom into the house probably recalls a time when it was usual to lay out the dead at home prior to burial. The hawthorn's sweet smell of putrefaction – which seems stronger as the flowers die – would have awakened painful memories.

Hawthorns are often characterised as being witch-like but they are more independent spinster ladies than wicked hags. True, they have no need of men, being bisexuals pollinated by their pet flies, but their pleasure harms no one, so it is their own business. They have a sense of fun and in spring they enjoy jumping out from the edge of woods, their blossom-laden branches raining down over their faces, like children dressed in white sheets out to give you a fright; but this is sprightly behaviour, not malicious. And they have a caring aspect. In the hedgerow, hawthorns will protect and raise an oak sapling, feed sheep and birds, and their berries and foliage will provide humans with remedies for high blood pressure and kidney and bladder problems. On the other hand, they will scratch you if you come too close, and yes, they don't change their underclothes as often as they might.

In the wild, we have two native species of hawthorn, the Midland hawthorn and the common hawthorn, though

Hawthorn: a tree of potent nostalgia, of old nursery colours and a whiff of sex and death.

there is little to tell them apart – the berries of the former contain two seeds, the latter only one. There are lots of local hybrids and pure Midland hawthorn is rare.

There is a naturally pink strain in hawthorn flowers which has been bred to prominence in several popular cultivars used in parks and gardens. The best known of these is Paul's Scarlet, which has double crimson flowers. *Rosea Flore Plena* is similar to Paul's Scarlet but more peachy, and Crimson Cloud has a fetching white eye in the centre of the red flower. They are all tough, stocky and attractive trees.

One of the strangest hawthorns is the so-called Glastonbury thorn which will blossom twice – around Christmas and again in spring. Devotees of the occult will know Glastonbury's reputation as the Arthurian Avalon, to which Joseph of Arimathea brought the Holy Grail after Christ's death.

The story goes that the Bristol Channel was bigger in those days and Joseph was able to sail some fourteen miles across the Somerset flats up to Wearyall Hill, where he disembarked and planted his thorn staff, which promptly flowered. The winter-flowering thorns of Glastonbury are still growing there. Glastonbury thorns can be bought from several nurseries. They will smell of summer when there is snow on the ground.

The thorn may be an import from the East, brought back by the crusaders. But we sometimes find twice-flowering hawthorns growing in our woods and hedges, so it might rather be a native variation.

Before barbed wire was introduced from America in the 1880s, a thorn hedge was the best form of stock-proof barrier. To prevent gaps in the bottom of the hedge it had to be laid or "plashed" every fifteen to 20 years. There are still distinct regional styles to plashing but the basic procedure is to cut two-thirds through the base of the stems, then push the hawthorns over and peg them down, like a line of fallen dominoes. This exploits a characteristic of trees known as "reiteration", whereby they will endeavour to regenerate, repeating their original shapes and reassigning their lateral branches as new upright stems. The result is a thickly multiplied, impenetrable hedge with many substantial cross pieces and barbed uprights.

Hawthorn is most commonly confused with black-thorn, with which it is frequently planted. Hawthorn wood varies from rough brown and silver through to red on the new twigs, but blackthorn has plum-coloured wood, often covered with a film of green moss. Its thorns are vicious two-inch spines and its fruits are sloes, the colour of blue-black autumn skies.

Blackthorn rarely imitates the twisted form of the hawthorn and left to its own devices will make a small spreading tree. Much of the time it seems barely engaged with the outside world. It has a nonchalance bordering on gloom and its leaves are sorry little spoon-shaped things that turn nicotine yellow in the autumn.

But in March, when woodland and hedgerows are still wet and dark, the blackthorn suddenly puts out blossom of startling rich cream. The flowers cluster thickly along the leafless twigs right up the spines, like swarming blossom-winged insects. A "blackthorn spring" describes the odd combination of flowers without leaves and cold March weather: a precarious, peculiarly British beauty. This is a performer that plays to an empty theatre. The flowers appear before walkers will be out to see them, while the sloes only ripen after the first frosts.

Blackthorns can be spitefully misanthropic. Although they contain no poison, their spines are horribly infectious, possibly because they snap off after entering flesh, lodging inside the body foreign matter coated with bacteria and bird-shit. (Blackthorn is also favoured as a larder by migrating red-backed shrikes, or butcher birds, who pass through Britain in spring and autumn and impale their prey on the thorns.)

Dog-owners will know the agony blackthorn causes in the paws of spaniels and labradors. In humans, blackthorns can cause mechanical dermatitis, cellulitis, abscesses foreign body granuloma, peritendinitis, tendinitis, peri-capsulitis, synovitis and septic arthritis. You should not ignore any injury from a blackthorn. Its glancing blow may be a coup-de-grace.

In its more approachable moments, the blackthorn is

also a contributor to the hedgerow shop and pharmacy. Sloes are rich in vitamin C. In the autumn, many tons of sloes are picked for sloe gin. But more often than not, sloes are collected on walks and then forgotten, a bagful of decaying good intentions. At the last minute it seems so old-fashioned to be making sloe gin and it has to be left for a whole year before you can drink it. In the past blackthorn leaves were boiled as a cure for laryngitis. Blackthorn was also a stock ingredient for commercial swindlers, who used the fruit to make "port"; while it was a jibe against grocers that their China tea had come from the leaves on the local blackthorn hedge.

Blackthorn is not the first hedgerow blossom of the year. Small wild plums, frequent along roadside verges, in ditches and the edges of woodlands, and more often little trees than bushes, come out into flower in early February and are often mistakenly described as blackthorns, though their white flowers are sparser and open alongside little green leaves. (Surprising to think there are insects around to pollinate at that time of the year.) Properly called myrobalan plums, they have many local variations and are relatives of the ubiquitous, early flowering purple cherry-plums in our cities. Their fruit makes good jam.

Any old hedge will have its share of elder and this one is no exception. Elder will travel a long way through a hedge in its quest for light. Here the pink and fawn-coloured stems, covered with pox-like blemishes, are up among the tips of the thorns, still pushing out some flaccid yellowing leaves, while the mother creature to these tentacles is far below and far away, a great stump that has been hacked to the ground an infinite number of times but shrugs off the assaults without a care. Elder never gives up and must be dug out to the last root.

Though it is a relation of the viburnums, the tough ornamental garden shrubs, elder is not an attractive plant. Endlessly variable in form, it will grow into a small tree but looks self-conscious when standing alone, as if unsure what shape to take. Often it ends up as a peculiar mixture of sweeping curves and brief uprights, like the ruins of an old staircase. It is happiest sneaking into the bottom of hedges and pushing aside other plants.

It is odd how elder seems to create a space, even in the most crowded circumstances. The other trees seem to move away, as if its presence were disturbing. Perhaps it is the body odour. The crushed leaves and wood of elder have a sweaty smell of oily, unwashed intimacy, though the flowers are quite different. In June, this shapeless and unpleasant oik turns into royalty, and is crowned by great flat white plates of lace-like flowers that produce a narcotic vapour, like mouldy cut grass and thickly sweetened lemon juice, that hangs like sleeping gas in low country

Blackthorn: a chilly precarious English beauty, which does its best work before an empty theatre

lanes. The surprisingly delicate cordial made by dunking the flowers – of which many restorative qualities are claimed – is just one of the elder products available from the hedgerow pharmacy. The plump little purple berries that follow the flowers are used for pies, juices and wines. They stain faces and clothes dramatically and are mildly toxic if consumed raw in excess.

Perhaps because of its protean nature and indestructibility, the elder, although dismissed by gardeners as an opportunistic weed, has been revered as the witch's tree to trump them all. There are numerous taboos surrounding it: like hawthorn, it is both lucky and unlucky. Some old farm-workers still refuse to burn elder because it is the residence of the Hag goddess or because it was the wood of the True Cross, or because the souls of the dead live in the pithy stems which generations of children have hollowed out for pea-shooters and pipes. In Ireland elder hedges were planted to keep away evil spirits. There is an old tradition that you should raise your hat to the elders you encounter on walks, and politely bid them good day.

This old hawthorn hedge also contains several species of large trees that were either planted with it or have sneaked in over the years – ashes and sycamores, and even one or two oaks, though the latter are still, by their standards, young trees. Left uncut, the hedge might one day turn into something resembling an ancient boundary.

The hedgerow is also the regular home of the field

maple, a discreet, charming little tree that rarely has a chance to shine out on its own and is ignored by the big-tree lovers. Alan Mitchell dismissed it as "depressingly moderate in all departments".

How unkind and untrue! In winter, it is a densely branched tree, with a milky-brown trunk scored with ridges and burrs like bee stings. It has upraised branches typical of maples and, like many maples, its structure of opposite twigs and leaves recalls the rigging and spars on an old ship. Balanced and poised as a ballet dancer, the field maple has exceptionally sharp and rusty autumn yellows and reds which go on into winter, after other trees have lost their foliage. In the hedge it can be harshly flailed – it can even be used for topiary – but left to itself it makes a tree up to 70 foot high. Field maples ignite the horizons of dull autumn afternoons, and make the roadside verges burn in a blur of fierce yellow.

The other common little hedgerow tree worth looking for is the English elm, which is sometimes presumed to have disappeared altogether. There are several of these in our hedge, whippy little things, scarcely thicker than a wrist, suckering from rotten stumps. The frail-looking twigs have a fish-bone pattern of shoots and tiny buds. Their bark is solemn and grey, occasionally puckered. Juvenile elms have small, pointed little leaves and might be mistaken for young beeches or hornbeams, but they turn rough and hairy and are a tired, dull matt-green until the sudden brilliance of their autumn yellow.

The elms here look shifty and furtive, as if they were trying to hide in a crowd, which is more or less the case. For the moment an elm emerges from a hedge and becomes a tree its fate is sealed. The elm bark beetle *Scolytus scolytus* has a cruising altitude above fourteen foot and will seek elms that stand out to feed on the bark. The beetles have a singular taste for the elm: they are also carriers of the fungal Dutch elm disease. As they munch and burrow, they introduce fungal spores carried on their bodies to the outer growth ring of the tree's wood. The fungus blocks the tree's water conduction system: the tree begins to choke and its limbs begin to die. The beetles then lay eggs on the tree and their larvae tunnel under the dead bark, becoming covered with sticky fungal spores. When the adult beetles emerge ready for take-off, they are already contaminated.

"Dutch" elm disease has been around since the early nineteenth century, but the older version of the disease was a less severe form, caused by the fungus *Ophiostoma ulmi*, also known as *Ceratocystis ulmi*. Early research on it was carried out in the Netherlands, hence the epithet "Dutch". The current epidemic dates from the late 1960s when a more virulent form of the fungus *Ophiostoma novo-ulmi* was introduced from North America in elm logs. Within a decade the adult elm population of England had been largely wiped out. Some areas were able to contain the disease by cutting down and burning infected trees. Brighton still has lots of big elms, though it recently cut down twelve huge diseased trees to be used as sea defences.

The fact that there are the remains of elms in this hedge means it has a history as a boundary and may date back at least a century to when the English countryside was still full of great elms. They dominated the hedgerows of the fertile midland plains, massive and straight with vast open crowns, more prominent even than the oak, topping the church spires visible across the flatlands. They fitted well with the non-conformist rural communities: severe, hardworking and practical. Farmers liked elms as boundary markers because they cast little shade on the crops, grass grew under them and they could be pollarded regularly for their tough straight wood. They also held onto their foliage late, which made it useful fodder for the animals, which were not put off by the hairy leaves.

In pictures and photographs the old elms have a lonely grandeur emphasised by the repetition of their forms. They elm had a distinct shape, because many of them were in effect clones.

The English elm has uncertain origins. It rarely produces fertile seed but reproduces by sending out lots of suckers. To plant a hedge with elms, farmers would simply use suckers struck off an adult tree. This method created a genetically limited elm population that looked similar –

and later shared a vulnerability to the beetle.

The best-known relation of the English elm is the wych elm, more common in northern Britain and in Scotland, a big blousy tree that often divides low down into thick trunks. While the bark of the English elm is smooth or cracked into plates, the wych elm becomes ridged and corky.

Wych elms have some lovely, floral touches. In early spring they put out little pink and purple flowers on their naked twigs, followed quickly by great clusters of almost translucent seed discs – or samaras – that shine along shady hedges and woodland margins like lurid green chrysanthemums. Though I have read that the name wych elm derives from the use of branches to douse for witches – those Victorians again – the name probably comes from the Old English word "wice", meaning supple. For the record, witches are supposed to shun elms. The tree has a special affinity with elves.

Diseased elms can regenerate many times from their stumps and suckers. The wood resists water and was favoured for coffins, so it is appropriate that the tree is a specialist in resurrection. Its life may be brief – just 20 years or less before the beetle comes to call and the cycle of dying and regrowing begins again. Still, the hedgerows are always busy with elms trying to beat death: you can see their yellow leaves, shimmering in roadside thickets late in the autumn. Some local species already show resistance to the disease. But in the meantime, if you have an elm and want it to live, it is best to keep it out of sight of the beetle. So cut off its head.

Bare essentials

HAWTHORN – Brown wood, sinuous, frequently "plashed". Thorns of variable size. White or blushing blossom in flat heads in May. **Lead red berries.** Toothy leaves like map of Britain with Cornwall missing.

BLACKTHORN – Black wood, vicious spines, **small spoon-shaped green leaves**. Creamy blossom before foliage in March. Dusty black and blue sloes.

WILD PLUM – Grey wood, small leaves that come out cucumber green alongside virginal blossom in February. **Fruit the size of a cherry**. Locally variable.

ELDER – Fawn-coloured pithy wood on protean bush. **Stinking anonymous leaves**. Huge heads of white flowers in June. Reddish purple berries.

FIELD MAPLE – Small tree. Pale brown bark, young wood looks prematurely old through creases. Many upright, fine branches with twigs opposite looking like the spars on a ship's mast. Toy maple leaves, acidic yellow in autumn.

ELMS – Whippy, upright grey-barked saplings, suckering from stumps. **Fish-bone pattern of twigs**. Hairy leaves. Tiny buds. Brilliantly melancholy autumn foliage.

5. *Forgotten Fruit*

A few yards down the lane the overgrown hedge breaks for a five-barred gate over which there is a clear view of the ruined farm buildings. They have a romantic desolation: all the evidence of industry, of an intense self-contained life now reduced to a few distinct, neglected details. There is a small cottage with a shed and outside loo, brick pigsties and a tumbled-down tractor shelter made of rusted galvanised sheeting. Rotting wooden posts, scorched black, and a few courses of sooty bricks mark the spot where a barn stood, until boys from a minor public school in the adjacent park burned it down while smoking and drinking cheap sherry back in the 1980s.

This small farm is held on an ancient tenancy agreement which passed down within the family when the last occupant died 30 years ago. By then the building was in need of serious repairs. The landlords – one of the larger Oxford colleges – dragged their heels, hoping to reclaim the tenancy. The family refused to give up their rights, and in the long stand-off nothing has been done. Curiously, it is now in the interest of both sides to let the place quietly fall down so that the cottage and pigsties, made from a rare local brick, will not be Grade II listed. One way or another, they can at least agree that the cost of putting up a new building would be a third of what it would cost to restore the current wreck. In this, the forces are with them. A local naturalist has identified the ruin as a nesting site for several rare species of bat as well as barn owls and little owls. Nesting owls cannot be disturbed but bats have an impregnable legal position as permanent sub-tenants. Under normal circumstances the presence of bats would cause horror in a householder wanting to do repairs, but they are happy news if you want to let the place fall down. Any tentative enquiry by the local authority as to the landlords' intentions is met with a stern reminder about the legal position on disturbing bats (six months in prison or a £5,000 fine) which is enough to put off most people.

If we climb the gate and go closer we can see that the yard has been used for tipping and there are piles of clay spoil, plastic drums and broken bricks scattered around. The whip-like stems of young sycamores and ash push up through the roof of the cottage: holly shields the front door. Elder and brambles have taken up the ground floor: a barn owl marks our progress silently from a hole in the old chimney breast. On the walls are scorch marks and obscene graffiti. The corners of the house are filled with bottles and shreds of old blanket and magazines.

Outside, something still survives of the proud and proper people who once lived here. To the rear of the house, among the wilderness of brambles and long grass, are half a dozen rows of old apple trees – short-trunked, spreading trees with knobbly, arthritic joints, their bark blue and green with lichen and moss and marked with canker and old pruning wounds. They have grown close together now and form low gothic arches with their branches.

An orchard never altogether throws off the ghost of cultivation and this one was planned carefully, planted with trees that would produce fruit from July until November. The branches of one row of trees are full of big apples, luminous yellow and green with faint flushes of red. Help yourself: I will. Yum yum. I don't know which the variety, but they are one of the thick-skinned autumn apples, the last phase of the crop that will hang on the tree until the depths of winter. The last apples are often the best – not the sweetest, but their flesh is firm and they have more flavour, a balance of sugar and acid over soft tangs of perfume. Yum. Oh yes. Nothing tastes as good as an apple scrumped from some forgotten orchard.

There are an incredible number of different domestic apple cultivars worldwide – some estimate as many as 20,000. In nineteenth-century Britain, at the height of the fashion for plant husbandry, there may have been as many as 7,500 different cultivars. Many old apples survive in forgotten orchards and only an expert could tell you the name of these wonderful fruits we are eating. How did one tree come to have so many offspring? The answer lies in its strange and exotic origins. You might expect the domestic apple to be a tamed version of our native wild apple or crab, a shaggy and sometimes thorny tree of wild and woodland edges. But the small, yellow, sour crab apples have little in common with the big, sweet and highly-coloured fruits of the domestic apples. The parents of our domestic apples may well have come from Asia, perhaps from the Tian Shan, a mountain range that extends 1,000 miles from western China through Kazakhstan and Kyrgyzstan to Uzbekistan. There, high up among snow-covered peaks and luscious meadows and cool forests, the domestic apple evolved courtesy of the sweet tooth of the brown bear.

It worked like this. The genes of the domestic apple contain proteins that prevent trees from successfully fertilising or being fertilised by identical trees (think how modern apples require the presence of a different pollinator for them to set fruit). Hence, apple trees always have the possibility of mutating. Many thousands of years ago the Tian Shan had huge fruit forests filled with an infinite variety of apples of all sizes and flavours. Brown bears prefer sweet apples, which also have the most fragrant skin (brown bears have excellent noses and can climb trees). And every time a brown bear scrumped a sweet apple, the seeds would pass through its gut, but not perhaps before 48 hours had passed and the bear had travelled a long way inside its territory. So, little by little, through the ages, the brown bear selected trees that were most fragrant, and the forest grew bigger and sweeter. Then men came along and quickened the process of selection, first by planting favoured seeds, then by learning the techniques of grafting shoots of sweet apples onto rootstock taken from another tree – a faster and more certain way of obtaining a fruit tree of a manageable size, since the final form of the tree could be controlled by the choice of rootstock.

Why the Tian Shan? In their recent book, *The Story of the Apple*, Barrie Juniper and David Mabberley have argued persuasively that the domestic apple arrived from China to the Tian Shan ten million years ago – just as the mountains were going up. (They are still rising today). The apple climbed on this natural elevator and rose high above the world, while below the deserts wrapped themselves around the feet of the mountains. For a long time, little could get in, or out, and the apple germinated and spread in cold, beautiful isolation.

Then, after the deserts retreated, apples were brought down from the mountains and carried west along the trade routes, planted both deliberately and through discarded fruit – rather as today you can see incongruous domestic apple trees growing on roadside verges, grown from cores flung from passing cars. Perhaps the domestic apple was brought to Britain by the Romans, or perhaps it was imported earlier by Celtic traders. Certainly by Tudor times we knew a lot about growing apples.

Apples are a wonderful food, rich in natural sugars, beneficial flavanoids and Vitamin C. (The pips do contain vitamin B17 which may form small quantities of cyanide – not harmful to humans but enough to deter birds from eating them.) They can keep for a long time – up to a year. Down the ages they have been pulped or dried, cooked or fermented into cider and brandy. (Juniper and Mabberley relate how, in nineteenth-century North America, country folk perfected the art of ice-distillation. A barrel of cider was left on the porch over winter: as it froze the ice was chucked out, turning modest booze into 66% proof "applejack". This natural method had the advantage of rendering open and "accidental" a process that was otherwise illegal.)

Apples are important not only for what they are but for what they represent. As they rolled through history they picked up and discarded all sorts of values, some scrupulously wholesome, others sensual or even wicked. To the Persians, Greek and Romans, the apple was a fruit of love with gorgeous curves and plump, sweet flesh and emphatically to be desired, though it might cause problems. The Trojan War began when Paris, asked to choose between the goddesses Hera, Athena and Aphrodite, gave the golden apple to the last.

The fruit's image was complicated by its appearances in the Bible, where it was integral to the Fall of Man. The apple – or what was presumed to be an apple – was rich not only in vitamins, but in potential sin, an idea reinforced by the confusing root of the Latin name *Malus* which may also mean "evil".

Thus apple cultivation came to have its religious connotations. It has been said that the popularity of apples in Britain is due not only to the climate but to Protestantism. It became the obligation of good Christians to plant and improve orchards, to graft and cultivate and generally by honest industry redeem the sinful fruit.

In 1653, Ralph Austen published his influential *Treatise on Fruit Trees*, which combined the insights derived from 20 years growing apples with chapters on "the spiritual use of an orchard. Held forth in divers similitudes between Naturall and Spirituall Fruit-trees; according to scripture and experience." In their spare time, clergymen grafted fruit trees as enthusiastically as they urged their parishioners to grow themselves upon Christ.

Not every Christian believed that grafting was acceptable, however. The most famous apple lover of them all, John Chapman or "Johnny Appleseed", who spread apple seeds across the north-west of America as he spread his unorthodox brand of Christianity, believed that "only God can improve the apple". In a way, he had a point. Many apple cultivars created by grafting proved to be short-lived as the process of grafting can make trees more susceptible to viruses.

In 1895 the Quaker chocolate magnate George Cadbury founded his model village Bourneville outside Birmingham. Each one of his tenants was supplied with a planted garden containing eight apple and pear trees and a plum. The gardens were to be maintained on pain of eviction. Cadbury's tenants were also given a handbook informing them that "apples are the most wholesome fruit; they should be used freely, both raw and cooked." (They were also advised to "breathe through the nostrils with the mouth closed, especially at night.") The love-apple of the goddess Aphrodite had been transformed into a health food that was the perfect cure for constipation.

Was the Biblical apple of the Old Testament actually an apple at all? It was very probably all a huge mistake based around some mistranslation from the Hebrew. The so-called Garden of Eden, that area of Mesopotamia from which the Genesis myths emerged, never provided the conditions for the germination of apples. Apple seeds require a prolonged cold period at temperatures near to freezing for successful germination to take place. These conditions prevail in China and central Asia and even in Europe, but not in Mesopotamia or even in Palestine, the site of several other supposed Biblical references to the apple. The apples of the Bible may be quinces or pome-granates, oranges or apricots. They may even be bananas.

Not quite the same image, is it, Adam and Eve sharing a banana? The Fall of Man might have been a comedy about a man and a woman, a snake and a banana. So you can tuck into your scrumped apple without feeling you are playing out any theological drama. Pity, really. What is stolen is always so much sweeter than what is given.

There is plenty of pagan mystery attached to the apple. Apparently, it represents a union of natural and supernatural forces. Cut an apple laterally to reveal the pattern of the pentangle: cut it vertically and its core looks like the female genitalia. And it has mistletoe, an essential part of the druid's kit. This beautiful parasitic plant, with its weird moon-coloured berries and pairs of identical, leathery, evergreen, sickle-shaped leaves, is spread by birds and grows on some 200 species of apple in Britain. It likes the rough bark and sap of poplars and limes but its strongest affinity is with old apples and it is common in the warmth and shelter of Herefordshire orchards. It was formerly detested by orchard owners, because it reduced crops, but it is now a valuable crop in itself.

Apple blossom bursts white out of pink buds, and it retains a carmine-streaked look in combinations as various as the trees. The pinks are deeper on the wild apples and some cultivated crabs, many of which are planted along our roadsides, supplementing the self-set domestic apples. When the roads of Britain are strung end to end with apple blossom, it is as if the pink is the stain of living blood moving along the arteries. We do enjoy the pink in our trees. Though this walk may seem already to be a journey of olfactory delights, what with hawthorn and elder flowers, the scent of apple blossom is better than any: delicate and inoffensive, honeyed and healthy, it brings shivers of vague, yearning hunger on a May morning. There is no dubious, rotting undertone: the scent is strongly sentimental, as if you had caught a whiff of some warm, comforting maternal body. Children seem to love apple trees – to look at, to smell, climb and eat from. From Homer through to Peggy Lee, artists have written and sung of the apple trees of their youth.

Not so long ago, our apples – indeed, all our fruit trees – seemed to be disappearing. Between 1970 and 1997, the United Kingdom lost 64% of its old orchards – more than 80,000 acres of apples. Hundreds of Orchard Streets and Orchard Closes are all that remain of these real orchards. It is not all glum news. There has been a resurgence of interest in apples and many old varieties have been rescued. The revival is partly due to the taste for cider, which uses blends of bittersweet and bittersharp fruit, such as the evocatively named Balls Bittersweet, Brown Thorn, Crimson King and Broxwood Foxwhelp.

The growing of apples may have been the work of good Protestants, but pears were the fruit of Catholic monarchs in France, where the cultivation of pears was a court art. Pears do not grow reliably in Britain. They need warmth and shelter and all too easily their fruit is malformed or drops in June. Pears are easily told apart from apples. The apple is a low-branching fountain; the pear is more of a water feature: it rushes upwards and sprays sideways, which suits it to espaliers and walls.

Old pear trees have a startled look to them. The branches are spiked like worn toothbrushes and the lead shoots are zip fasteners against the sky. The pear's jerky, upraised character becomes more exaggerated the more it is pruned. Old pear trees seem to be features of many city gardens: their fruit may be cankered and woody and their bodies split and failing, but this only makes their flat heads of white blossom seem more pure and spectacular, as if they were always young at heart. Old pears also do sterling service holding up washing lines.

If there was a pear here in this orchard it has gone: perhaps it was planted against the wall of the house and has rotted along with its protector. There are some plums, spreading, untidy trees, with purple-black bark, that have suckered and hidden themselves in a small forest of thorns growing from the blackthorn rootstock on which they were planted. Plums only ever seem to be tentatively tamed trees and yearn to go wild. Their blossom is white and should come out in April, shortly before the pear and a whole month before the apples.

It makes a man itch to stand in an orchard like this and see it go to wrack and ruin. Think of all that gorgeous wasted fruit falling to the ground every autumn to feed the wasps and slugs and blackbirds, while we drive to the supermarket to buy bags of tasteless woolly apples from the southern hemisphere.

We are suckers for the colour of supermarket apples. Biologists have struggled to explain the evolutionary necessity of the joyous red gene in apples. Bears, for example, cannot see colour and therefore it is technically no use for an apple to be red, since this will not make it noticed. But humans do see red: our eyes are drawn to red, it excites us. Supermarket buyers have worked out that red apples attract humans irrespective of their taste. So ultra-red apples are bred to attract the gullible.

If you want to plant an apple, think small. Apples come in varying sizes – dwarf, semi-dwarf and standard – depending on the kind of rootstock on which they are grafted. A tree on dwarf stock will give you 50lb of fruit a year: a huge old standard tree may bury you under 400lb of apples, but it may measure 40 foot across and you will spend much of the autumn up a ladder, if you are up to climbing ladders by the time the tree reaches maturity. Anyway, why spoil the day with thoughts of productive labour? Why not take another sweet, stolen apple from this tree? It may teach us nothing of good or evil, but it will tell us what a decent apple can taste like.

Old pears are useful to hang your washing from.

Bare essentials

DOMESTIC APPLE – Low, spreading tree like **stumpy pillar** in gothic church aisle. Graft marks. Mossy grey bark. Pink buds and white blossom. Wild apples in verges bold pink and white blossom.

DOMESTIC PEAR – Upright, spiky, jumpy appearance. Long vertical shoots droop. **Short spurs** on twigs look **like zip fasteners**. Black square-cracked bark. Strongly scented white blossom. Wild pear spiny but rare.

PLUMS – Spreading, variable. Dark ruby or purple bark, often split. Lots of suckers. White blossom.

Revision quiz II

1. **Blackthorn flowers**
a) In May, after the foliage
has come
b) At Christmas
c) In March on naked
branches

2. **To plash my hedge I
would**
a) Pee on it regularly
b) Bring bits of it into the
house on May morning
c) Cut it halfway through
and lay it flat to encourage
reiterative growth

3. **Field Maple is**
a) Depressingly moderate
in all departments
b) A charming hedgerow
tree with brown ridged bark
and brilliant yellow autumn
colours
c) A spreading shrub with
rancid foliage

4. **Elder is related to**
a) The viburnums
b) The syringas
c) The Joneses

5. **English elms were
formerly propagated by**
a) Striking suckers off and
planting them
b) Seeds carried by beetles
c) Brighton and Hove local
authority

6. **Mistletoe is most
commonly found in**
a) Oak, ash and beech
b) Apples, poplars and limes
c) Norfolk, Suffolk and
Essex

7. **Which witch is wych?**
a) Hawthorn
b) Elder
c) Elm

8. **Apple blossom shows as**
a) Pure white flowers in March
b) Carmine-pink buds and white flowers in May
c) A hint of magnolia around the coving

9. **Dutch elm disease is spread by**
a) *Ophiostoma novo-ulmi*
b) *Scolytus scolytus*
c) *Scritti Politti*

10. **Hawthorns have**
a) Brown stems and red berries
b) Black stems and sloes
c) Black stems and blackberries

11. **Wych elms have profuse bunches of**

a) Flat, round seeds cases called samaras
b) Triangular seed cases called samosas
c) Overlapping branches that shade out other trees

12. **Which of these are old varieties of apple?**
a) Miss Milliewhips, Crimson Snowdrift, Transparent Quince
b) Balls Bittersweet, Brown Thorn, Broxwood Foxwhelp
c) Royal Wave, Blushing Bride, Queen of Hearts

Answers: 1a 2c 3b 4a 5a 6b 7c 8a 9b 10a 11a 12b

6. *An Art of Darkness*

After leaving the orchard, a few minutes' walk down the rough track brings us to a small tarmac road, smeared with mud from tractors. The footpath sign tells us we should go right, along a narrow verge which sweeps down into a dip and then up again. Above us looms a country church, its lower areas fading into a shadowy mass of dark foliage.

The church's height is exaggerated. It sits up on a bank, looking down at the old rectory across the narrow road. The farm buildings, visible from the track we took, are further along the road behind a low brick wall. The church is a grey, square Norman church, one of countless such unpretentious buildings, their exteriors crusted with lichen, their interiors smelling of damp and worn varnish. All but abandoned, the church has wrapped itself round with consolatory peace drawing into its body a population of house martins, bats and owls. Every second Sunday of the month the door is opened to the congregation. A handful of people come to support the local vicar, a decent sort who keeps an eye on the older parishioners.

The vicar lives in a bungalow nearby. The rectory across the road is a handsome castellated, red-brick folly sold by the church in the 1960s, and has long been owned by keen gardeners, who have partially restored the topiary for which it was known in the nineteenth century, when a High Anglican incumbent had a passion for sculpting bushes. After his death the gardens were vandalised by locals confused between topiary and popery. Much of the iconography created over a lifetime – the hearts and crosses, the mother and child, the twelve disciples, peacocks, castles, dragons and birds – was chopped down overnight. The current owners have not achieved the same razor-like definition of form that divided the old clergyman from his flock: proper topiary requires trimming and bud-nipping all summer and half the autumn, and all by hand, for hedge- trimmers will take a bite out of a leaf and leave the rest to discolour. But they have managed cones, balls and spirals and an avenue of swans leading to the front door. Actually, the swans look a bit like chickens.

There is an air of mystery to the shapes of plants trimmed to unnatural lines or imitating the forms of living creatures. If anything, the topiary in this garden is more perplexing than it must have seemed when it was all perfect, for now the shapes are less determinate, more artistic than actual. The balls are less than spherical, the cones are unequal sizes. The idolatry has gone: now the topiary is a bridge between the domestic and the wild, deferring to both worlds and belonging to neither. A hazy waking dream, filled with unintentionally erotic geometry.

Topiary is an old art: the Romans brought it to Britain, and they probably learned it from Egyptian and Jewish slaves. If properly treated, many plants can be shaped, including rosemary and juniper. The topiary of the ancient Mediterranean and North African countries must have smelled wonderfully savoury. It has often been a discreet iconographic code, a recusant art, into which its creators locked some secret of their hearts. After the Romans, topiary was saved by the great monasteries, where gardens were planted as spiritual allegories, and found its way back into popularity during the Renaissance. In Elizabethan England, the knot garden, parterre and maze were expressions of a complex social dance, while on the Continent, topiary was recruited by the state. The gardens at Versailles contain a great army of cones and balls – a statement of virile power and wealth, a marvel of monotony. The trees are cut to a uniform size and shape with templates. Even the horse chestnuts are squared off.

During the eighteenth century, British topiary took a more individual turn and grew in eccentricity, until the formal garden was swept away by Capability Brown's "natural" landscape. Topiary was loathed by the Romantics: it was such bad taste to see nature so tortured. By the time topiary was again fashionable in the late nineteenth century, many magical gardens had been lost. In 1729, a yew at Harlington church near Brentford was clipped into a spectacular arrangement of cones, globes and weather-cocks. A century later it was once again a shaggy yew, in which form it continues to this day.

Alexander Pope, himself an important horticulturalist who instructed garden designers to "consult the genius of the place", was no fan of topiary. In 1713, the *Spectator* carried his satiric "A Catalogue of Greens", in which Pope mocked the manner in which the dramatic ambitions of the topiarist were regularly thwarted by the perversity of nature. Pope's list of putative designs included:

> Adam and Eve in Yew; Adam, a little shattered by the fall of the Tree of Knowledge in the great storm; Eve and the serpent very flourishing.
> Noah's Ark in Holly, the ribs a little damaged for want of water.
> The Tower of Babel, not yet finished.
> St George in Box; his arm scarce long enough, but will be in a condition to stick the Dragon by next April.
> A grave Dragon of the same, with a tail of Ground Ivy for the present.
> NB These two not to be sold separately

The topiary in our rectory garden is made from box

and yew, both long-standing favourites in ornamental gardens. Both are evergreen native trees. Box can sometimes be found growing wild on chalk hills as a shrubby tree. A significant problem with using box in hedges and topiary is the increasing occurrence of "box blight", a fungal infection that causes death and discolouration of the foliage. Blight is encouraged by the leaf wounds caused by trimming so topiary makes the plant more susceptible to disease and there is no treatment, except to cut it out as soon as you see it.

For this reason some gardeners now prefer to use common privet instead of box in hedges. Privet is fast-growing and can be closely cut, but it is not a perfect substitute; it is only semi-evergreen and the longer, softer leaves do not give the same neatly defined lines as the small, bright green or gold small oval leaves of box.

Yew makes superb topiary, and the best hedges. (It is not as slow-growing as is widely believed and may put on six inches a year, once established). However, it has an entertaining reputation for being deadly poisonous to living creatures and preferring the company of the dead. Big yew trees are not much tolerated in open countryside, where they might be grazed by livestock, and are found mostly in old gardens and graveyards like the one in which we now stand. For some, the yew will always be a tree with a chilly reputation, a ghoul with its fingers down among the bones, its intense shade dry and musty like an enclosed room. But on this bright winter afternoon, what could more beguile any miserable thoughts of mortality than the green of the shaggy old yews clustered protectively around the quiet grey of this Norman church, spilling their shade out across the crooked tombstones and sunlit, rabbit-cropped grass?

Thus displayed, the hereafter looks coolly tranquil. The dead are a vital part of the present scene. Why care about what you can have so little control over? And yew is such an egalitarian tree. William Cobbett called it the "English Cedar". The size of the cedar of Lebanon makes it of use only to the wealthy – it is a tree of Biblical kings – but anyone can sleep under the yew.

Believers in Celtic arcana revere the yew as the earthly embodiment of the divine consciousness, but there is no evidence to support the stories of its pagan significance, which are largely based on the assumption that many churchyard yews are thousands of years old and mark ancient religious sites adopted by the early Christians. In practice it is hard to calculate the age of old yews because there is no definite series of annual growth rings to study. Instead, a fungus, *Leitiporus sulphureus,* turns the inside of the tree into a mass of soil-like rotted wood. Old yews often go hollow. One vast, hollow yew at Leeds in Kent

Topiary: a vague dream, filled with unintentionally erotic geormetry.

was said to have been lived in by a family of gypsies. But size is no guarantee of age. In 1987 the naturalist Oliver Rackham measured a yew at Hatfield Forest as having a girth of fourteen foot and seven inches, but concluded that despite its size the yew could be no more than 230 years old, dating from the time the grounds were redesigned by Capability Brown.

Yew is long-lived and some of the churchyard trees throughout Britain are arguably between 1,000 and 1,500 years old. The yew's ability to resurrect itself from an apparently dead stump makes it particularly suitable for the Christian churchyard, though we simply do not know if yews were planted for symbolic reasons. In Wales, which has a wealth of ancient yews, many of the local church-yards are said to have associations with early saints, suggesting that yews provided shelter to hermitages before the churches were built. But Christian literature contains few references to yews, while the Anglo-Saxons do not seem to have credited it with any significance other than as a cure for the "water-elf disease", which is thought to have been measles.

So that early association between yews and churches remains a riddle. Perhaps some yews were planted on royal orders to shelter churches, and later, more yews were added to maintain an uncertain tradition. Wordsworth, who immortalised the ancient origins of the Borrowdale yews in Cumbria ("those Fratenal Four... joined in one solemn and capricious grove"), planted several yews in the churchyard at Grasmere. From the eighteenth century many of the yews planted near churches were Irish Yews, an upright "fastigiate" form that originated in Co Fermanagh with the characteristic shape of a crumbling, many, towered sand-castle or less grandly, a jelly-mold. Yews certainly like the environment around churches. Gardeners are recommended to feed yews on "blood and bone". And oddly, yew wood is blood red at its heart.

Whether or not they speak of the life to come, yews are considered a definite danger to living creatures. But it is not, interestingly, the tempting little red berries or "arils" that pose the greatest risk. (The flesh of arils can be eaten: it is the pip that is toxic.) The poisonous taxine in yew is concentrated in the foliage, and a handful of leaves would do serious damage to a child. Taxines will cause nausea, vomiting, palpitations, inertia, coma and death. There is no cure except rapid purging, and sufferers of yew poisoning should be taken to hospital immediately. Technically, yew is so toxic that in an age when local authorities quail at the thought of litigation, it is surprising that the tree still stands in parks, and schools are allowed to have them on the premises. In 2005 Bristol County Council removed a row of yews that had only just been planted because they had been advised the trees posed a risk to the children in a nearby public play area. The decision was widely mocked. Is the yew a needless target in the elimination of potential liability? Or are we complacent?

We live alongside thousands of natural poisons that cause us little trouble. The Royal Horticultural Society lists around 100 common garden plants, shrubs and trees that are to some degree either poisonous or an irritant. Some of the most cheerful of our garden companions are on the list: horse chestnuts, lords-and-ladies, autumn crocus, lily of the valley, daffodils, hellebores, bluebells, wisteria, snowberries and privet. Some have fruits every bit as enticing as the berries of the yew. Perhaps we should ban the lot of them.

Humans have learned to be conservative about what they choose to eat. Since children are most at risk from poisoning, it is the business of parents to pass on this knowledge. Arguably, this didactic thread is an important bond in the relationship between adults and children. If you eliminate risks, you alter this relationship.

Anyway, in Britain there has not been a case of fatal yew poisoning since records began in 1963. Over the past two centuries only a handful of deaths have been noted and these include suicides, psychiatric cases and a mother who apparently killed her three children by feeding them yew foliage as a cure for worms. In America a ten-year analysis of 11,197 cases of suspected yew poisoning showed that in the vast majority of cases there were no ill effects or only minor gastrointestinal symptoms. In just four cases were there life-threatening effects. There were no fatalities.

Cut yew foliage is more deadly because the poisons become more concentrated as the leaves dry out. And yet those same taxines can be extracted to provide innovative treatments for breast cancer, so the tree has saved human lives rather than taken them.

It is true that many livestock have died from eating yew foliage, but the effects are by no means predictable. Horses and pigs are probably most susceptible: cattle and deer less so. Sheep have been killed by yew, but some breeds of primitive sheep seem to be able to eat large quantities of one's prized hedge. Deer eat it also. It is thought that deer may get a "kick" out of eating yew, since it acts as a heart stimulant, rather like a double espresso.

Our path goes through the graveyard round to the rear of the church, but before we move on, let us cast one loving, envious look back to the perfection of the old rectory. A pity it is not the summer, because then they open the garden and there must be other tree treasures round the back. In fact, there are in the front garden a few smallish trees worth a mention, poking over the topiary balls. Two deciduous and one evergreen. And a low, untidy bush with a few small rotten apples hanging from it.

The trees are not old ones, but recent plantings, in excellent taste, though one of them is also a salutary lesson. It is a thin, pallid tree, seven or eight foot tall, slightly orange on its narrow stem, dividing into several weak, dehydrated-looking twigs that point outwards and upwards with vague hope. It could be a young maple that has lost its way – not a pretty tree, the young black mulberry.

It is worth quoting a couple of great dendrologists on the subject of the mulberry. Alan Mitchell – of course – wrote that it "has no place in a book devoted to inspiring and noble specimen trees as it has never managed to make anything of the kind". John White, who filled Mitchell's boots as his successor dendrologist at the Forestry Commission observed that "few trees can claim to be as rewarding in cultivation as this one".

Mitchell was outraged that anyone should be fooled into thinking that the mulberry, which everyone loves for its gnarled and twisted, ruined-antique look, and for the way it reclines full length on the glistening front lawns of stately homes, while handing out the fruit all summer long, should be mistaken for an ancient tree. He was himself fooled once or twice and it galled. No tree could outsmart him! He snorted at the idea that Shakespeare had planted a mulberry that was still living or that Milton had once dozed under some twisted mulberry and argued – convincingly – that trees which were thought to be more than 300 years old had scarcely qualified for their pensions. They looked old because of the traditional means of propagation. This involves using "truncheons" – five-foot branches – which are hammered into the ground in autumn. The branches quickly root and bush up. Hey presto, an instant old mulberry tree! It has a short life, is covered in great welts and burrs, never grows more than about 30 foot and spends most of its time on its back, basking in attention and admiration.

As White wrote, doubts about its aged "appearance" should not detract from the sensuous pleasure the tree gives. When it begins to fruit, the berries fall like sweet purple rain. Unfortunately, if you buy a little mulberry in a little garden centre pot, propagated by a little cutting, it may take a good chunk of your life to get going, and this is what has happened in the rectory garden. The tree has been labouring away for six years already and may have another ten to go before it pops out a single mulberry. In the meantime, it is not pretty. It is not anything much. In summer it has those languid, long, tongue-shaped mulberry leaves, but it is so unsatisfactory. We don't want to wait sixteen years for a mulberry! If you must have a mulberry you need to buy an old house with one in place – either that or find yourself a five-foot truncheon.

What am I?
Tulip or gingko?

See page 254

The other deciduous baby poised among the topiary is a similarly slender tree with curved, gently descending boughs. This is a Judas tree which will never grow hugely tall. It will tend to spread and weep, though it can be cut back and managed in a small space. When spring comes, great clusters of pea-like purple flowers— more a kind of superior Chanel rose-pink – will dangle from the arches of its branches before the round leathery leaves appear. On older trees, with dark and gouged bark, the flowers sensationally appear directly from the wood, like some kind of coloured exhalation from the awakening spirit of the tree. It is a streak of colour in the spring, an exotic visitor flashing through the garden, clutching her Lulu Guinness bag with brilliant felt colours stuck onto black velvet.

The name is supposed to reflect the improbable legend that Judas hanged himself from this cheerful tree; but Judas is probably a mangling of Judea, indicating an eastern origin. One surprise is that the flowers have no scent, but if they did it would almost certainly be overwhelming or disappointing. The colour is enough to set the imagination going. How we love pink! But this is a classy pink.

A choice evergreen tree shields the front door of the house. At first you might take it for a bay tree – one of those from which you get the big leaves for cooking – the large, glossy, aromatic shrub that can be shaped into a spire. Like the bay, it is bushy with serrated green leaves but it has dangling strawberry-like fruit. They are rosy pom-poms that hang in clusters and take two years to ripen, so the tree generally has a few on the go all the time.

The fruits are not toxic but taste nasty, and the Latin name is *Arbutus unedo* meaning "I eat only one." So perhaps they are usefully didactic so far as small children are concerned. Go on! Help yourself, and you'll never pick another strange berry again! The fruits will still be there when the tree blooms in summer, with clusters of white flowers looking like the weird berries of the mistletoe.

The strawberry tree has an eccentric natural range that encompasses Cork and Sligo in the West of Ireland, Lebanon and Israel. In Britain it rarely exceeds 30 foot and is an essential on the garden list. The young bark is brown to orange; and the hybrid strawberry tree has yet more beautiful reddish bark that looks like highly polished mahogany.

That messy old bush with the rotting apples is a medlar. Every posh garden requires a medlar, just as they need a mulberry. It is an old fruit, related to the rose family, that comes from the East and has been grown here for centuries. There is nothing dramatic to look at: small, pear-like leaves arranged attractively around pleasant, large white flowers that smell of cucumber and Pimms and hard, squashed-looking brown fruit. The fruit are horrible to taste until they are "bletted" – broken down by frost, like sloes – and then they smell horrible but taste interestingly acidic. You can see the point of it in ages when fruit was in short supply in winter, but these days it is for people who like their Camembert very runny. If at a country house your host jovially offers you a medlar after dinner, demand to know if it has been properly "bletted". Such opportunities for embarrassing guests are all some people have in their dotage, and it is why they cling onto their medlars.

The footpath goes down the side of the churchyard, between straggling bushes of holly interspersed with self-set yews. There are broken-down thorns which rise through the rough piles of gravediggers' marl, hung with shreds of plastic bouquets and dead flowers. From these shrubberies the adjacent farm is visible: behind it a grain silo, a Dutch barn and long, low sheds, viewed through a row of Lombardy poplars. Even in winter the form of these tall trees is as tight and dense as the slender rocket shape of evergreen cypresses: they look like the bars of a cage. The writer Miles Hadfield described them as "a notable exclamation mark in our scenery". They shout across the fields in uncanny unison, because they look uncannily identical.

The true Lombardy existed only in a male form and so the tree was propagated by cuttings, with little genetic variation. However, the male Lombardy poplar seems to have hybridised with other common poplars to produce a female version.

This common tree does look very different. It has an open crown, rather like a sky rocket with its nose blown off. A disputed variety, "Plantierensis", is said to look similar to the male Lombardy, but is even denserformed.

The male Lombardy is not in fact a great feature of the landscape of Italy. It was introduced to Britain in the seventeenth or eighteenth century, possibly by an ambassador to Italy, and is now used to front shady activity, lending spurious Continental grace to the scrap metal dealer and the intensive chicken farmer, a cheap Italian suit for those on the make. It grows with furious speed and many of the older trees, planted when it was still considered something graceful and rare, have been cut back severely. One common substitute is the beech Dawyck Gold, which also grows tall and columnar but is altogether subtler with spring foliage a bright gold-green. There are also several cultivars of the so-called cypress oak that look like Lombardies, but they will generally be found in a better class of park.

There are many species and hybrids of poplar less noticeable than the Lombardy, and poplars are omnipresent, if mostly unremarkable, features of shelter belts along roads and around towns. As solitary trees, poplars may be hard to spot but they stand out as a crowd, particularly in winter when the upright lines and feathery crosshatching of many commercially planted varieties seem drawn across the more flowing and irregular lines of other trees, like the shading on a landscape drawing. The effect is rather Continental, reminiscent of the French countryside, glimpsed from a passing train.

Some of the more characterful poplars enjoy the company of willows and like them, can be found growing thickly along verges and riversides. The sprawling, burred and gnarled native black poplar has an old stronghold in Buckinghamshire, and the naturalist Richard Mabey describes wonderfully the "exotic orange glow" in the Vale of Aylesbury, when the low afternoon sun of March strikes the glossy new twigs of pollarded poplars, with their "ochre bark and ginger-shellacked buds".

Other distinctively coloured poplars include the black poplar hybrid "Robusta", which has leaves that are chocolate-purple when young, like rum-and-raisin ice cream. Great stands of these thunderously brooding trees have been planted and make it look as if autumn has arrived before spring has got underway. The white poplar has pale bark which is easily confused with that of the silver birch, though its trunk is patterned low down with black diamonds like puckered kisses. It also looks similar to the aspen, a relative of the poplars and one of the first trees to colonise Britain. The aspen is known for its habit of quivering as if it had a dose of malaria. The stalks on its leaves are weak and flat so that the leaves respond helplessly to the slightest breeze. Poplar leaves generally flap loosely and the trees seem to churn in the wind, briefly changing colour when the leaves' silvery underside is exposed.

At the rear of the churchyard are the remains of old iron parkland fencing and one of those wicket gates that allows a body to slip through but keeps cattle at bay. Beyond, the path turns slowly back towards the dual carriageway. It descends across an open meadow, and then runs alongside a ruined wall and a gloomy belt of dark trees, above which rises the soaring spire of some monumental evergreen. This we must see.

Bare essentials

BOX – Evergreen, small, stiff, pale green oval leaves with a central crease. New growth yellow at the edges. Occasional small wild tree. Frequent as hedge or topiary. **Suffers from blight**.

Lombardy poplars: a screen for a seedy enterprise.

YEW – Evergreen. **Low shaggy, dark green** with upswept branches. Foliage: long "needles". Small yellow flowers in February. Red arils. Bark and wood are red.

MULBERRY – Always stout. Older trees monstrously deformed, with twisted black wood and vast bosses. Mostly falling over. Big terminal buds. Big leaves. Purple fruit.

JUDAS TREE – Spreading, low, branches like arches. **Black cracked bark** on old trees. Pink-purple flowers come directly from wood before leaves.

STRAWBERRY TREE – Superficially like bay. Serrated, glossy leaves. Clusters of strawberry-coloured fruit. White flowers like mistletoe berries.

MEDLAR – Shrubby. May still have rotting brown fruit in winter with jellyfish look to them. Wide, loose white flowers in spring smell like garden party punch.

NATIVE BLACK POPLAR – huge gnarled tree and burred tree, often sweeping with orange new twigs. Now very localized.

HYBRID BLACK POPLARS – tall trees with repetitive, feathery fishbone effect of branches. Like cross-hatching on the landscape. Some Hybrid Black Poplars such as x *canadensis* "Robusta" have spring foliage with striking, thunderous autumnal colours of purple and orange.

LOMBARDY POPLAR – Rocket-shaped, upright spire dense even in winter. Female Lombardy poplar has a more open crown.

WHITE POPLAR – Silver underside to leaves that look like small version of a maple's. White bark with diamond patterns like puckered kisses.

ASPEN – Creamy bark kissed with diamonds. Looks like white poplar but later into leaf. Leaves serrated cogs on long, flat stalks.

Do you know me?

See p254

Dangerous trees

Despite recent panic that has seen many old trees
removed because of health and safety implications,
trees are rarely lethal in themselves. Tree-related
deaths are connected with exceptional weather
conditions – when old trees blow over – or with the
annual "self-pruning" that mature trees perform.
They may shed 10% of their branches each year –
more if stressed by lack of water. But from 1998 to
2003, there was an average of just six tree-
related deaths a year, or one in ten million of the
population. There is, however, one tree continually
associated with anguish, discontent and violence,
the Leyland cypress, x *Cupressocyparis leylandii*.

A natural hybrid between Nootka cypress and
Monterey cypress, this appeared in Ireland around
1870. Hardy, fast-growing and sound-absorbent, it
was widely used to screen roads and railways – in its
place a thoroughly useful plant enjoyed by birds,
but lethal in suburbia where it has come to play a
pivotal role in boundary disputes. It can grow more
than three foot a year, gobbling up the light, rising
vertically in a dull green wall 100 foot high, like a
wave rearing ominously from the flat seabed left by
a retreating tide. Two or three years of neglect and it

is away, beyond the reach of the ladder and shears.

It is, in the words of the *Collin's Tree Guide*, "the most planted and the most hated garden tree". Ten years ago it was claimed in Parliament that there were some 17,000 hedge disputes in Britain, many of them involving leylandii. The publicised cases varied from terrifying to bizarre. For longevity there was Stanton v Jones, a dispute that began in 1971, when Stanton, who was a pensioner, planted a leylandii hedge. When the hedge reached fifteen foot high, Jones began complaining. By 1977 it had reached 25 foot high. A persistent, bitter row evolved, involving solicitors, tape measures, hedge-cutters and chainsaws. Jones twice lopped the hedge: Stanton sued for £32,000. In 1996 Jones won permission to trim the hedge to twelve feet. Stanton, who was pushing 90 years old, promptly planted another leylandii in his garden...

Then there was the case of the midnight piddler, the Lincolnshire pensioner who took to urinating on his neighbour's leylandii hedge in an attempt to kill it. (The build-up of urine crystals may block conducting vessels in young trees.) In Northumberland, a couple were said to have spent £25,000 on legal fees to have a hedge cut down. In Newbury shots were exchanged and in Powys a man was murdered after a long-running dispute about leylandii.

A class of people evolved who styled themselves "hedge-victims" – a description that implied that they were subordinate in some way to the overwhelming evil of a tree that commanded one person to plant it so that it might abuse another. "Hedge dispute counsellors" appeared, charging £70 an hour... In the end legislation was deemed necessary. Under section 6 of the Anti-Social Behaviour Act 2003, aggrieved parties may ask the local authority to reduce the size of a hedge.

To plant this tree in a hedge will be seen by your neighbour as a considered provocation, the announcement of your intention, at some point in the future, to pick a fight. The Leylandii is more than just a means to secure privacy. It allows you to enjoy the fantasy that next door does not exist. Those on the other side feel they are being wiped out by sterile shade. But anyone who plants this kind of hedge is defacing themselves. When we cannot see our neighbours, they cannot see us either, and we become monstrous in their minds.

Leylandii quickly grow out of control

7. Elephants, Whigs and Scottie Dogs

L awson cypresses have a distinctive smell, dry and sour, neither offensive nor altogether pleasant. It is slightly antiseptic and numbing, like long-dried herbs found in a jar on a kitchen shelf. Planted in thick belts, these cypresses provided shelter for the Victorian ornamental gardens, and though they never grew as fast as their distant relatives, the Leylandii, have since, the shadow of the Lawson is every bit as formidable.

We are among Lawson cypresses now. That intimidating shade seen from the higher ground of the churchyard turns out to be a thick barrier of the trees, planted in two rows behind a low estate wall. Our footpath runs down the side of this, across fallow fields towards the dual carriageway, but the wall is no obstacle, no more than a few tumbled-down stones, and there is no attempt to keep people out. Under the tall Lawsons the ground is dry and bare. The shelter seems popular with birds, which flit to and fro down the alleys between the trees. Some of the Lawsons are shading each other out and their foliage is tired and brown, but where they stand in the light they rise up ramrod straight to 40 foot, their foliage billowing around the stems like dark green smoke. Their bark is dry and flaking like bad rough skin.

Maligned by association with the Leylandii, the Lawson cypress is not half as miserable as we assume when separated out from a crowd of its fellows. Cypresses can be slightly creepy because they have no twiggy structure within the foliage – the foliage is by and large the structure – so they are flobby and boneless, but used in conjunction with deciduous trees, their bold shapes prop up a garden throughout the weariness of the winter. Tough as old boots, easily transplanted and growing from seed that germinates in just three weeks, the Lawson is indispensable in and out of town. Sooner or later, even the greatest tree snob needs a Lawson. "Garden planning in Britain is primarily the study of Lawson cypresses," observed Alan Mitchell. "Other plants are just infilling."

Like many of our ornamental evergreens, the Lawson is a massive forest tree in its native environment of Oregon and California, where high rainfall, the moisture from Pacific sea fog and mild inland climates created a magical land of woody giants, now one of the last refuges of the great trees. The Lawson makes good durable timber (the Japanese apparently used to pay vast sums for the tree as coffin-wood) and is used as a nurse in forestry plantations in Britain. But its principal employment is ornamental.

Seeds were sent over from California in the mid-nine-teenth century. Planted at the Lawson Nursery in Edinburgh, they initially produced green progeny, but fairly soon the trees were popping up in all sorts of different shades and colours, until the current list of Lawson cultivars is comically long. There are gold Lawsons and silver Lawsons, variegated trees, weepers and creepers, spreading cones, pillars and domed bushes and mini-Lawsons that do bum-clenched sentry duty in the front gardens of houses great and small. But the basic shape is a tall, tight spire, with that extraordinary cypress foliage: the tiny, flat leaves joined together like insect segments to form fronds resembling the patterns left by worms when you lift up a stone. There are no twigs to speak of, just glutinous foliage – much bigger and less feathery than that of Leylandii.

This belt of Lawsons mark, the perimeter of the old gardens and parkland once attached to a grand house whose occupants owned most of the neighbouring land. These days the house – a small Georgian façade with large Victorian aggrandisements that has done its stints as mental hospital, war hospital and failed public school – is divided up into separate flats and wings, and the parkland is currently the subject of a planning application which would, for phase one, permit the erection of 78 detached executive homes, with a strip of affordable housing boasting views of the dual carriageway. An access road has already been pushed across this former field of dreams.

Chalk white, it comes straight as a hammer blow from some southern corner of the park, where it connects to a discreet sliproad. The chalk track cuts between clumps of trees, crossing the lime avenue, before stopping abruptly among the neglected grassland. There a digger is parked, waiting complacently for the inevitable consent.

The lime avenue: this is something you have only glimpsed in passing, through all those years going up and down the carriageway. There, at its southern extremity, are the gateposts – without gates – that are visible from the road. The big stone piers taper towards their tops, where they are abruptly snapped off. Whatever stone animals once crowned them have been removed. But from the gates, up to the distant bulk of the house, is an almost unbroken, double line of limes half a mile long, trees that seem to mirror each other in their gently declining branches and the bushy red growth erupting within their canopies.

Limes are both some of our oldest native trees and some of our most prominent aliens. There are three principal species of lime in Britain, but in winter they can all have the same fundamental look of elegant deference. Their branches weep, not so thickly as the ash, not so untidily, but in short, composed bursts of polite sadness. The environmental scientist and author Peter Thomas elegantly describes them as looking like a series of connected rainbows, because the lead shoots tend to fail and each new shoot comes from underneath the preceding twig, so that the structure is like a series of swags. In practice, the effect is often more angular, busier and cruder, particularly with the common limes which make up this avenue.

Our natives limes are the Broad-leafed and the Small-leafed lime. You rarely ever see the former in the wild and large colonies of the latter – a dainty shimmering tree in summer – are restricted to a few precious, charming old woods in the east of England. The small-leafed lime is sometimes called "pry". In the National Arboretum at Westonbirt there is a closed circle of pry, formed from the suckers of some massive root system thought to be the remains of a 2,000-year-old tree. The common lime seems to be a hybrid of both broad-leafed and small-leafed limes, and is hardly ever found in the wild. However, from the seventeenth century onwards it became one of the most planted of ornamental trees and research suggests that most of the originals came from Holland, where this particular species is now rare. It is an exceptionally strong hybrid and the Dutch nurseries discovered

And me?

See p254

that it could be quickly and cheaply propagated by "layering" – encouraging the tree to set its lower branches in the ground where they would soon form clones. Many thousands of the Dutch-grown limes were imported to satisfy the fashion for the lime avenue, and many more were later used to bestow some class upon the expanding city suburbs. We are still planting common limes now.

In research published in 1992, Donald Piggot, then director of the Cambridge Botanical Gardens, argued that there are in fact two distinct clonal groups of Common Limes, both originating in Holland, one of which grows more conically than the other, tends to have the crowded, sprouting growth within its canopy and to shoot more vigorously from the bole. It is in short, a whiskery sort of lime. The other clonal group produces a tree that is more gracious and well-behaved, a mixture of upright stems and descending boughs, though it is often tarred with the same brush as its untidy brother. So common limes are the Cain and Abel of the tree world. From personal observation, this makes sense: there are avenues of common limes that sucker and spread very little, while others are uniformly rampant.

Why lime avenues? There is an old saying that Whigs planted limes and Tories planted oaks, but it also crops up as Tories planted limes and Whigs planted oaks or Whigs planted limes and Tories planted elms. The rising popularity of lime avenues certainly coincided with the revolution of 1688-89 and the ascendancy of William and Mary. Bearing in mind the origin of both royalty and tree in Protestant Holland, it would seem that whoever bought limes from the Dutch might be making a statement of alliance. The big Whig landowners and merchants were more inclined than Tories to support a Dutch Protestant monarchy over the incumbent Roman Catholic James II. One would not, I suspect, suggest planting a lime avenue on the site of the Battle of the Boyne.

Under William and Mary there was considerable redesigning of Hampton Court, including the planting of thousands of Dutch-grown limes in formal avenues. So arguably, the widespread introduction of the common lime into towns and country estates marks the adoption of a new formal taste influenced not by France, but by Protestant Europe, a civilised taste, which was to become associated with such prominent Whiggish voices as Alexander Pope, poet, satirist and gardener.

On the other hand, people who cared not a joy about fashion or politics planted common limes because they were cheap and healthy and grew fast, and there was an obvious, uncanny, military uniformity to the clones. It was like having your own guard of honour lined up the drive. The common lime remains a foreign mercenary and will never shake off its functional aspect, but in summer it can also be a deliciously attractive tree – in the right place. In the city it is now more often than not a problematic bastard with its rampant growth and aphid groupies, but given space in a park its heart-shaped leaves provide cool drooping shade, the June flowers are nectar-scented and the yellow autumn leaves have a feisty melancholy. The bark is dark, almost black, and its vivid red twigs are also apparent in the basal shoots. If you have one of the bad brothers it can prove a high-maintenance tree. If not looked after they quickly become unkempt – indeed the limes in this avenue could do with a haircut and a shave. They are suckering furiously, and in summer they will be smothered in foliage without any of their boles visible. These bear the mark of Cain, which is not how a good Whig should look.

To either side of the avenue, the parkland is dotted with groves of horse chestnuts and sweet chestnuts, unrelated trees and both introductions which have nevertheless become a treasured part of our vision of old England.

There is something elephantine about a horse chestnut. In winter its big limb has a parabolic fluidity, like the trunk of an elephant that has just plucked a small sapling from the dust and is about to stuff it into its mouth. The bark is also like hide, sometimes cracked like a baked potato, but thick and grey and flowing. There are few straight lines in a horse chestnut, however massive it grows. If you come close enough you cannot miss those big sticky buds with their prominent scales. Nothing that looks even vaguely like a horse chestnut has sticky buds.

I think of the horse chestnut in elephantine terms also

to remind myself what an outlandish tree it is, one that has become so planted without being of much practical use for its wood. And yet we love the conker tree.

A native of southern Europe, it was introduced into England in the early seventeenth century, possibly by the plant-hunting Tradescants of south Lambeth, and was an immediate success as a fast-growing ornamental. It makes an excellent shade tree for hedgerows or for parkland and is an easily grown and faithful companion to many lonely homes. About the first tree of substance to come out in spring, its huge, ragged-edged, tear-shaped leaves turn banana yellow as they drop in the early autumn, and for many will always be associated with the return to school. In recent years many of the horse chestnuts across the south of Britain have been afflicted with leaf-mining insects that cause early shedding of foliage and sometimes almost total loss. "Our trees are dying" scream the headlines. No cause for panic. Leaf miners are common and trees can generally make a full recovery the next season. More serious is the "bleeding canker" that can affect the tree.

Under the prettiness this is a cunning creature. Just as the oak has built the jay or squirrel into its plans, so children are clearly part of the horse-chestnut's strategy. What

The horse chestnut, standing guard like a faithful dog outside the isolated house.

it is to have such a glossy, attractive, coveted seed, easily pocketed by children! Squirrels and jays forget where they have stored their acorns and children drop their conkers and tread them into the mud where they germinate easily. There must be thousands of households with a conker tree growing in a pot, but many more who have one or two that have set themselves tight next to the secure shelter of a house and its inhabitants. A self-set sycamore or ash is regarded as intolerable, but a horse chestnut is welcomed for sentimental reasons, though it is at least as threatening to the foundations of a house, grows in a hurry and can top 100 foot. If it can survive six or seven years without being removed the tree will start to flower, at which point the prettiness of its white candles will plead, often successfully, for its life.

The candles of the horse chestnut are hyacinth-like stalks of white flowers tinted pink inside. They shine out, bobbing up and down against the vast wobbling form of the tree, like lights upon the ocean or night-time at one of those concerts where everybody is obliged to hold up a lighter. It is a great show, visible over the fields and far away. The tree carefully ekes out its blossoms for much of April and May, opening a few flowers at a time to make sure that all of them are pollinated. If pollination is successful, the flower develops a crimson tint to indicate to insects that their job has been done, a task which requires great efficiency. This tree is no dumb beauty. When several horse chestnuts are planted together the picture is bizarrely two-dimensional because the spacing and pattern of the candles seem regular as wallpaper. The effect is even more pronounced with the muted colours of the pink or red horse chestnut, which is a great favourite in towns.

There is something of the cuckoo about the horse chestnut. It wheedles its way into your heart, and then it looks after its own interests. Horse chestnut wood is useless even for burning and while conkers are said to have been used as fodder, they have been known to cause paralysis in animals and severe illness in children. There is even one recorded instance of death in a young boy, though he had eaten a prodigious number of conkers. Horse chestnut is also one of a number of trees known to secrete allelopathic phytotoxins, chemicals that restrict or even kill its competitors, and nothing much will flourish around a conker tree. If none of this persuades you to remove the sapling growing in the wall border, then think of the smell. One not much discussed drawback of the mature horse chestnut is the smell of its flowers. Perhaps you too have been at a party on a summer evening when everyone is trying not to remark on the unequivocally rude and unromantic smell of an adjacent tree – though not everyone dislikes it. I have heard it described as being "a bit like peppermints".

If you have the space to plant a horse chestnut, then think of planting the Indian horse chestnut. Not as blowsy as the usual conker, the Indian horse chestnut is less rapidly ascendant, more widely spreading and has infinitely more interesting foliage. This comes in luscious shades of green and bronze in the spring; the leaves are smaller and glossier and the autumn colours are better. The flowers emerge later in the summer so are not lost in the crazy rush of our modern springs and they also have different tints, of white and crimson with flecks of yellow. It gives you fruits as well, sleek black ones, but later in the year again, so that even in winter there are sleek black conkers to pick up and put in your pocket.

No relation of the horse chestnut, the sweet chestnut – called in olden days the Spanish chestnut – does not produce worthwhile nuts in Britain, just mangy little semi-hemispheres for the woodlice and wildlife, but it has long been grown both as an ornamental and for its strong but easily split wood: it can be coppiced and cut for poles at between eight and fourteen years, depending on whose advice you take. There are great areas of sweet chestnut coppice in the Forest of Dean and the poles are still sold, in much reduced quantities, for pit props.

Often passed over in the list of grand British trees – not native, you see, came over afterwards, probably with the Romans – it is a long-lived beauty that with age acquires the most distinctive bark of any common tree. While the bark of most of our other major hardwood trees is cracked or ridged horizontally or vertically, the red bark

on the fat boles of an old sweet chestnut is gouged diagonally in great curving lines that give the look of a fair-
ground helter-skelter or – in the adult version – the back
of a malingering sailor, half-flayed by great swipes of a
cat-o'-nine tails. This is the tortured tree.

In Britain, sweet chestnuts can often live 500 years,
rivalling the oak for antiquity. There is a famous tree at
Tortworth in Gloucestershire thought to be at least 900
years old. In their native Mediterranean they live much
longer and one legendary tree on the slopes of Mt Etna in
Sicily was said to have had a girth of 204 foot, and to have
been planted well before the birth of Christ.

Despite its mangy nuts, there is some evidence that
sweet chestnuts were previously planted in Britain for
their fruit. Certainly they were once present in much
greater numbers. In past centuries the rural poor were
encouraged to roast and grind the nuts up to make chestnut flour, a practice which is making a faddish return, but
the possibility that the nuts once grew big enough to justi-
fy the planting of great chestnut orchards makes one wonder if far back the climate was warm enough to produce
not only the grapes the Romans grew, but nuts to rival the
marrons of the Continent. Such thoughts are consolatory,
not for the prospect of free food if the earth heats up, but
because they show that we have lived through it all before.

In winter, along with the old bark, the new twigs are
also a handy guide to identification as they are reddish and

have flat, fluted sides. Come summer the sweet chestnut, despite its size, looks neat and glossy and spiked, rather like a holly (the leaves stand proud rather than droop) and the rounded canopy glitters and bristles confidently from a distance. In July it unexpectedly produces catkin flowers that look like huge, trailing, yellow caterpillars. They can smell sickly, and some think the smell is much more creepy than the flowers of the bonking-conker.

To admire the great twisted bark of the sweet chestnuts we will have to venture out from the cover of the Lawson Cypresses and risk discovery, but there is no one around to shout at us and the perspective is worth it. Standing in the middle of the lime avenue, we can appreciate the design of this earthly paradise: the clumps of trees arranged in casual formality like guests at a party, some screening the house, others inviting the eye to travel onward into vistas of forest and meadow, some of them sheltering low mounds of rising ground, one of which is topped by what looks at a distance to be a large concrete bell, but is the remains of a temple dedicated to Pan. Look at the dramatic confidence of the avenue. That sudden swamp-like hollow is all that remains of the dew pond. There was also a lake, but it has long since been filled in with rubble. What a fine sight it must have made for the owners in the eighteenth century, looking down from the house across this managed wilderness, grazed by sheep or deer, the quintessence of Whiggish good taste.

And yet there is something not altogether restful about the park. Perhaps it is the flayed bark of the sweet chestnuts that sets my mind running, or that military air of the avenue. The place, so calm and spacious, seems to hover between repose and action. It has a memory of violence. I have it. It is like a battle plan. Here are the troops, the Dutch mercenary limes, streaming from the house in a double column, bristling with twiggy confidence, while down one of them from the left charge the imported Mediterranean mastodons, the massed horse chestnuts, stamping and thrashing with their great grey hooves and huge swinging trunks while the Spanish chestnuts lie crosscut and wounded on the grass.The lime twigs stream with gore. The Lawsons, spectral visitors from the future, stand sentry in mute, dull respect, enclosing a battle that has gone on for 200 years. They sweat slightly with the effort, like guardsman do.

Perhaps some Georgian couple were the conquerors of this field. Perhaps they talked as they trotted through it, planning how they would spend the money earned from sugar or spice or slavery on a new lake, or a ha-ha, or perhaps on the latest fashion for planting dead trees to romanticise the fringes of the park. And should they have one of those new-fangled cedars: but, dear husband, do they yet grow well enough in our clime? What is the word from London?

There is a cedar of Lebanon in this park, up the northern end of the lime avenue. We do not have to go closer to admire it, because even at a distance it has such a dominant presence, both physically and aesthetically. If a spreading oak is a piece of living engineering that declares the strength of the tree, the cedar of Lebanon is a monument that shrugs off its weight. Sometimes an upright, star-scraping spire, at other times it can look like a hugely magnified bonsai. This is the latter sort. It is imposing yet exhilarating, a pagoda temple with a flat crown topping the 80-foot structure. The sparse but massive branches spread laterally, leading to dependent flat islands of luxuriant dark green foliage that clothes the structure like great folds of silky green cloth. As it sayeth in the Good Book:

> Behold the Assyrian was a Cedar in Lebanon, with fair branches, and with a shadowing shroud, and of an high stature; and his top was among the thick boughs. His boughs were multiplied, and his branches became long. The Fir Trees were not like his boughs, nor the Chestnut trees like his branches, not any tree in the garden of God like unto him in beauty.
>
> Ezekiel XXXI

A thrilling portrayal of a tree, and of a nation. Jehovah

An old sweet chestnut – the flayed look of its lacerated bark.

quickly smote the fair Assyrian to the ground, but the words remain resonant, for even to this day there has ever been much smiting between the Assyrians and the Israelites over who should own the cedars of Lebanon – certainly not the Lebanese.

There are two other sorts of cedar we should know about, the Atlas or Atlantic cedar, and the Deodar. They grow to the same size and can even have the same spreading habit, especially if pruned. There is an old rule for telling them apart– the mnemonic LAD. The foliage on the Lebanon is level: on the Atlas it ascends; on the Deodar it droops.

While this is mostly useful, they can at times imitate each other – an average Lebanon can look very like a decent Atlas and vice versa – and unless they are all alongside one another it is hard to pass judgment as to what constitutes significant upswept foliage tips on a tree the size of an office block. Also, while the Lebanon generally has the darkest foliage, it sometimes comes out blue-grey, like some variants of the Atlas.

If our imagined Georgian couple did plant a cedar, they were probably disappointed. The tree was introduced in the late seventeenth century but most of the first plantings were killed by the vicious frosts of 1740, the like of which were never seen again until 1962. The planting of the cedar of Lebanon as the mark of established wealth really took off in the early nineteenth century, when the trees successfully grown in this country began to show their hardiness.

In this period no grand home was complete without its cedar. The 1832 edition of Loudan's *Useful and Ornamental Planting* concluded that "no tree confers such an air of grandeur and dignity upon the grounds surrounding a mansion as a full-grown cedar of Lebanon". However, purchasers should be aware that "no check should be opposed" to its spread by planting with other trees as if it were wild: if you were a man of taste, and decently rich, you showed it by letting the tree spread. "It will never abound but in the seats of civilisation," concluded Loudan. Remember that: a squashed cedar is a sign of unaffordable pretensions.

A mark of wealth during a man's life, the cedar allowed its owners to take their status to the grave and beyond. When the London Cemetery Company opened its graveyard at Highgate in 1839, the centrepiece of its extraordinary necropolis was the Circle of Lebanon, the best address in the afterlife, a subterranean circle of family mausoleums under the sheltering bough of a cedar.

Of course, the Highgate cedar cannot have looked as impressive then as it does now, but all the same, cedars do not necessarily grow slowly. The Atlas cedar, introduced in the 1830s and a native of the mountains of Morocco and Algeria, is a quick grower and its offspring the Blue Atlas, a naturally occurring variation introduced a couple of years later, is a dangerous combination of beauty and vigour. The pale blue-grey foliage is so tranquil, so soft looking, and the habit is so gentle as well as big. It is a large teddy bear, a tree hugger's delight, a tree that bespeaks moral integrity in its grandeur and kindness in its colour. The tree is tolerant of pollution, indifferent weather and poor soil. It is very tempting but a mistake to put it in the garden and imagine that it will be someone else's problem. A Blue Atlas planted near Powis Castle in 1892 grew 80 foot in under a hundred years. It is quite common to see suburban houses disappearing behind the soft-blue Sesame-Street monster planted out front. You have to admire the sheer courage of some people.

The Deodar is a Himalayan tree, sometimes sacred but also used for construction and ship-building. In addition to the drooping foliage, it is distinguished by a conspicuous, pencil-straight trunk running right up through its canopy. In Britain, it was frequently used for windbreaks and was also touted as an alternative to the oak, but the wood never grew strong enough. In general, cedar wood, sweet-scented, resistant to decay and handy for deterring moths, has never been available in Britain in useful quantities. To grow well here it needs a lot of uneconomic space.

The cedar of Lebanon is not the tallest tree in this park. If we look behind, back to where we sneaked in, back to the shade of the Lawsons, we can see rising up above their canopy that huge sharp peak we first glimpsed from the churchyard. It must be at least 100 foot, an evergreen spire with sharply hanging branches. It is a clue that somewhere in the jungle of the shelter belt is the remains of the park's pinetum – that Victorian showcase for the great evergreen discoveries of the cool and misty Pacific North-West and the pines of the hot Mediterranean.

The pinetum turns out to be little more than a glade or two among the shelter trees, where under distant circles of sky, some very tall trees with few lower branches stand on soft, scented ground crackling with needles. It is not exactly thrilling. Pines and conifers are not as fashionable as before, no longer exotic. The big deciduous trees preoccupy us and most other evergreens are lumped together in our minds with Christmas trees and Forestry Commission conifers and dark German forests where the natives live off chocolate gateau and do unspeakable things to foreigners. Besides, telling pine trees apart often involves counting needles and sniffing foliage, all of which is cruelly dismissed as stuff for the anoraks.

There is no time to debate the taxonomy of spruce, pine, fir and cedar. Many trees have changed names and categories several times or have two names, so let us just look at one or two select species that are still growing in this park. First we need to clear up the Christmas tree question.

There are no Christmas trees growing here. The management company that owns the place chopped them down, removed the tops and sold them to the local council a few years ago for town centre decorations. But for the record, a Christmas tree is a Norway spruce and the telltale signs are very short, spiny, dark green leaves – or needles, if you must – which have faint white lines up their sides. It has been planted in Britain for at least 300 years and there are at least 350 different cultivars. Available in blue or grey or pale green, sweeping or spire-like, it can be a very pretty tree. Its use for Christmas is down to Prince Albert, who posed the Victorian royal family around a decorated tree for a seasonal portrait.

It is most confused in the popular mind with the Sitka spruce, the mainstay of high-altitude Forestry Commission plantations. As mentioned before, the Sitka spruce is by some way the most planted tree in Britain, but it does not look pleased with the fact. Aye, 'tis a woeful tree, a dour-looking thing. No doubting its toughness or its usefulness in supplying cheap timber and paper pulp, but it never looks joyous, even when – as here – it is rescued from the miseries of the close-packed plantation and grown on as a big specimen.

The one in the pinetum is perhaps 70 foot, which is nothing to what it can do given the rainfall of Scotland. There it can easily top 150 foot. Its spare blue-grey foliage hangs in weary clusters on widely spaced branches. The base of the tree is grey and swollen like an old bottle, as if it had become the wino of the woods with a sorry tale to tell about his childhood among the nameless multitudes. The tree has filled out at the bottom and grown at the top, but there does not seem to be much in between: the shape has disappeared, as have large areas of foliage. It has flat leaves, very stiff, spiked and unwelcoming. The side leaves are perpendicular to the shoot but the upper leaves are slanted forwards like a twist of barbed wire. Love me or leave me, it says, chop me down if you must but don't touch me. I don't like people touching me!

So we chop it down and slay it in multitudes. The virtue of Sitka timber is its strength relative to its lightness, which makes it useful in the building trade. In North America, where the best-quality timber grows, the tree was used by the Wright brothers to build the *Kitty Hawk*, in which they made the first powered flight.

It continued to be used in aircraft production during both World Wars and was a major component in Howard Hughes' amphibious *Spruce Goose,* the biggest aircraft ever to have taken off. Surprisingly for such a dour tree, you can strike a jolly tune from its light wood and it is used in the sounding boards of violins and guitars.

There may be a reason for the depleted look of the tree we see here. To do presentably, Sitka spruce needs as much as 30 inches of rain a year. It sure likes the bottle. The gloomy tree in the pinetum has probably had enough to drink in the past, but the dry summers of recent years must now be having an effect. Climate change may make life interesting for the Forestry Commission. Hitherto, Sitka spruce has prospered in the north and west of Britain, but less rain may make its future less certain.

The Sitka spruce was first described growing in Washington State in 1792 by Archibald Menzies, the Scottish surgeon and naturalist who sailed with George Vancouver on his exploratory journey up the north-west Pacific coast. Forty years later it was another Scot, David Douglas, who saw the potential for the tree – that it would grow on poor thin soils where the Scots pine would not – and shipped the seed back to Britain.

Douglas is a hugely important figure in the evolution of the British landscape, responsible for many essential trees in the Victorian pinetum. He was deeply in love with the mountains and the trees of the Pacific North-West. His interest was not really in pretty ornamentals for the garden, but in the introduction of species with commercial potential to the wet climate and impoverished soils of his native Scotland. It is to him that we owe the introduction of the Douglas fir, the tallest timber tree of them all.

And indeed it is the immense spire – really an Apollo rocket – of the Douglas fir which forms the centre of this depleted pinetum. If we stand back, we might reckon that this tree is, say, four modest houses high, at least 120 foot, but this is half the size of the tallest one in Scotland, a third the height of the tallest one known in Oregon, and just a quarter the height of a monster 415 foot tree that is said to have been felled on Vancouver Island in 1902. Imagine that! Four hundred and fifteen feet, the height of clouds, the height at which a light aircraft might beetle to and fro across the countryside: a little under a third of the height of the former towers of the World Trade Centre. We should not be impressed by size alone – humans are forever putting up tall buildings to commemorate short-lived egos – but a living plant, 415 foot high! How did they fell it without it smashing a hole through the earth's crust?

The rivals to the Douglas fir for height are the redwoods, the coastal redwood and the sierra redwood, known to us as the Wellingtonia. Neither of these is present in the pinetum – perhaps a huge rotting stump there marks a Wellingtonia that succumbed to fungus many years ago – but they are often found together in ornamental gardens in Britain, and a quick digression is essential to sort out their differences, which are the cause of much head scratching and family dissension.

Generally lumped together as "sequoias" the Redwoods are natives of the Pacific North-West of America, where they both grow to preposterous heights. However, on their own massive scale, they are like Laurel and Hardy. The coastal redwood (*Sequoia sempervirens*) is able to draw on the extra moisture contained in the sea fogs of Oregon and California to boost its recorded height to more than 360 foot. Inland, up in the mountains, the sierra redwood

(*Sequoiadendron giganteum*) generally grows a hundred foot less but puts on a vast waistline instead, producing a spreading, massively buttressed, red-barked spongy bole. The bark looks similar to that of the coastal redwood but it is softer and the timber is also spongy and useless, while the coastal redwood has proved all too useful and has been largely chopped down. (It can, however, regenerate from a stool, like a giant's coppice tree.)

Side by side, the leaner, more aspirant nature of the coastal redwood is obvious, but when are you ever going to have the correct perspective to view them together? It is always a case of too close or too far. Hence, anorak or not, you will have to peer at foliage to be absolutely sure, and their leaves are completely different even to the most short-sighted. The coastal redwood has leaves not dissimilar to those of the yew, but the sierra redwood has frondy tails made up of little scales, looking like wimpy asparagus.

The sierra redwood was successfully propagated in Britain in 1853, a decade after the coastal redwood, and was named Wellingtonia in memory of the Duke of Wellington who had died in 1852. This was a canny sales move, which ensured the tree was required planting for estate-owners, who had already got over the thrill of owning a cedar of Lebanon. Yes, that rotting stump was surely a Wellingtonia.

Oh – the third redwood. There is another redwood, but

this should only be a confusion of names, not of appearances. This is the dawn redwood – hardly a key feature of any Victorian pinetum as it was only identified in 1941, although it is everywhere now, even in many mid-sized gardens, and its popularity requires some explanation.

It is a deciduous conifer like the larch, and thought to be one of the oldest of living things. How old I forget. Very old. At least 100 million years, and beyond that things get vague. Fossils of it have been found and it was thought to be extinct until lots of trees were discovered up the Yangtze, where it was so common it was used as cattle fodder. Also called water-larch, it is sometimes muddled not only with the redwoods but with the swamp cypress, which is a thrilling and sinister tree that pushes up root nodules in the water and breathes through them, like crocodiles' noses. (You can see them at Kew.)

The dawn redwood caused great excitement in the wake of the Second World War – it was like a postcard from the past, conveying some shred of future hope to an otherwise gloomy world. It proved to be easily propagated from seed or cuttings and was planted throughout many western countries. It is generally a conical tree, with a rigidly straight red-barked trunk and a flared bole like 1970s jeans. The leaves are like the yew's, but it is deciduous, remember, and in autumn it flicks some internal switch and pulses orange and red before vanishing, like the Tardis, for the winter. If in December you see a one-legged, flare-trousered nude yew with a bizarrely conical shape, you are doubtless looking at a dawn redwood. Or a dead yew.

It is peculiar how, standing at the base of a big Douglas fir, unable to comprehend its size, I have sometimes found myself on other days talking to other people about anything but the tree beside us, as if my mind were blanked by the immensity of the immediate subject. When you get into this giant's world, it is all about vast size or tiny detail. The closer you come to the tree, the less you see of it. There is no medium-shot; most of life just seems irrelevant to this scale, and so you stand under the space rocket and wax philosophical, though you can talk about the ugly bark.

In its maturity the Douglas fir has characterful bark to match the redwoods – basically like the face of Pete Postlethwaite in any one of his recent bad-skin, 60-a-day appearances: craggy, ridged and mottled with pale orange. The foliage, hanging in elegant, pendant boughs, is made up of soft, gentle, dark needles that grow all round the shoots and smell delightfully of grapefruit when they are crushed.

The Douglas fir is arguably the most important commercial timber in the world. It is the only thing to use for lasting exterior woodwork on a decent house and commands a hefty premium. When imported it was formerly known as Oregon pine and was standard on new Victorian houses. Drill into a Victorian lintel and the smell of the forest wood is fresh and fruity. The Douglas fir needs more protection and fertile soil than the Sitka. You will find plantations of it on the lower slopes of Scottish mountains, or in the south-west of England, sometimes growing alongside western red cedar, another giant from America which is easily told by its glossy, green, immaculate, worm-patterned cedar foliage. Like the Douglas, this has a distinctive fruity scent, described by some as like pineapple, so on warm days the valleys and mountain slopes of Britain can smell like an opened can of Del Monte pineapple and grapefruit cocktail.

And what about the pines? We cannot overlook the pines, those delicious-scented trees, even the shabbiest of which can make you feel clean, and which are so emblematic of particular places and yet so disregarded. The most obvious in this collection is our native Scots pine, among the most romantic of all trees, a dashing adventurer that looks windswept even in cosy situations, restricting its foliage to a few lofty, spreading crows' nests parked at irregular intervals up its slender trunk.

Why is the symbol of Scotland a thistle, when it should be the Scots pine, which seems to grow everywhere without ever losing its love of the hills? It is forever dreaming of bad weather, longing for the roar of the wind through its needles, the damp mist on its skin and the clatter of rain on its unprotected head. The unusually good looks are due in part to its striking mix of colours, which also incorporate a couple of essential Scottish features. The bark is a characteristic smoked-salmon pink that may be more prominent further up the tree and the foliage is blue-grey as the beadiest of Scottish eyes.

This is the second-most commonly planted tree in Britain. Most of them are in Scotland, up the mountains being grown for "red deal" – rough red wood for fencing, paper pulp, palettes and packing.

The other easy-to-tell pine is a tree with a clean, slightly inclined trunk and distant, rounded canopy, just like an umbrella. This is indeed the umbrella pine, the Mediterranean tree most people are familiar with from their holidays, which leans out over old seaside towns and new golf courses, and which is often planted in Britain as a reminder of an ideal retirement destination.

Some of the other pines here have subtler characteristics. The Austrian pine is a thickset thug with rough resinous bark that can look almost tar black. It is common as a shelter tree. But more widely used, and often found in now uneconomic plantations, is the Corsican pine, a slender and monotonously simple tree: everything about it – bark, foliage, cones – looks grey, as if it had been splattered with dust. It bespeaks long and weary servitude in a

**Scots pine: forever dreaming of bad weather,
longing for the roar of the wind through its needles.**

lost cause. It does smell nice, but on clear autumn days the Austrian pine is worth a longer sniff.

The obligatory contribution from the Californian coast, and yet another David Douglas discovery, is the Monterey pine, the most cheerful of pines, with brilliant green soft needles and an occasional habit of sprawling in a laid-back manner, with a number of big stems. Despite its beach-bum manner, it can grow very big and it is in fact a rare example of an imported tree doing rather better over here than in the wild, where it is bizarrely restricted to a hot, narrow strip of Californian coast around Monterey.

Robert Louis Stevenson stayed in Monterey in 1879 and is said to have used it as the setting for *Treasure Island* – the sites, sounds and pine-rich scents of the book are redolent of the area. David Douglas, always in a terrific hurry and not given to seeking pleasure, admitted to the seductive beauty of this aromatic part of California, which was in his day still Mexican.

He got along speaking classical Latin much of the time he stayed there as he was passed along a long line of hospitable priests. Douglas tended to reserve his poor sight for staring at plants and trees, but even he weakened in the presence of the Californian girls. "If ever I had a kind feeling for man's better half, I left it in California," he wrote. The Beach Boys did not put it better.

I have studiously avoided talking about cones, though they are one of the ways of distinguishing the evergreen mob – Douglas honed his marksmanship shooting cones off high trees – but the cones of the Monterey pine are worth mentioning because they are hard little fire-resistant hand grenades that can stay on the tree for many years. In their native groves, the cones are said to open simultaneously in the wake of natural fires, and the seeds fall with a terrific spooky rattling. Picking up cones to light your fire is a classic pastime for families renting a forest hideaway. Don't even try to burn Monterey cones. They will not burn.

We should move on. The day is passing and there are trees to look at when we get back to the city. Who knows, the next time you come to this park perhaps it will be to look at one of the houses. Will it be one of the three bedrooms along Lime Walk, or the more exclusive address available at the Cedars, or perhaps a plot with a swimming pool among the Chestnut Groves? Fat chance of that. Too bad. Perhaps the planners will ensure that most of the trees survive to plague the incomers with their roots.

Let us saunter boldly across the park back towards the dual carriageway. There we can pick up a path that runs along the roadside embankment and wander back to the lay-by. It gives us a chance to pass through those imposing gate-posts, as if we were walking out of a film.

Just by the edge of the dual carriageway are a couple of solitary trees we must stop for. The first is deciduous: naked, sleek and grey, pendulous and deferential yet grave.

Too tidy to be British royalty. A handsome foreigner – a classical hero? Possibly.

Like the sweet chestnut, the common walnut may have been brought here by the Romans, who may have had it from the Greeks. It has a statuesque quality and foliage superficially similar to that of the ash. However, the dark glossy leaves come out very late with a triumphal rosy glow to them and have a rich, sweet, oily scent – half-offertory, half furniture polish – when crushed. Possibly this tree is the self-set offspring of a long-gone grove, for in earlier centuries home-grown walnuts were jealously prized for their fruit, which are these days inevitably stolen by grey squirrels.

The other tree is an evergreen, a tall green sentinel with lax foliage. Let us test your new knowledge. What is it? Yes, it looks like a Lawson cypress, but the branches do not smell sweaty, the bark is coming off in an odd gluey mess and when you hit the trunk it goes ping.

This is the modern version of profitable estate planting, a mobile telephone mast disguised as a cypress. It is made of steel tubing covered with fibreglass bark decorated with plastic foliage and costs, so they say, about £36,000.

Bare essentials

LAWSON CYPRESS – Tall, evergreen spire. Flat foliage like insect segments and worm tunnels. Not feathery like leylandii. Sour, dry smell.

COMMON LIME – Red new growth. Abruptly ascending or **zigzag twigs**. Suckering and shooting.

HORSE CHESTNUT – Elephantine shape. **Baked-potato bark.** Fat, sticky buds.

SWEET CHESTNUT – Tortured bark with horizontal gouges. Unexpected catkin flowers like huge yellow caterpillars in July.

WALNUT – **Fit Greek god** with aromatic ash-like foliage.

CEDAR OF LEBANON – Ideal form is huge, **round-topped bonsai tree** or pagoda with flat islands of foliage. Bark dark brown.

ATLAS CEDAR – Should have upward-inclined plates of foliage smaller than those of the Lebanon (bring one along for comparison). Bark is paler, grey. Blue Atlas has grey-blue foliage.

DEODAR – A less spreading tree, but very erect. The foliage drips or droops.

NORWAY SPRUCE & SITKA SPRUCE – One makes a pretty Christmas decoration: the other makes the wrapping paper. Short, stiff leaves versus very spiny leaves arranged like **twisted barbed wire**.

DOUGLAS FIR – Old trees straight and narrow with tight, upswept, tufted and teased foliage. Leaves are soft needles all round shoots that smell like grapefruit when crushed. **Bark like Pete Postlethwaite's face.**

COASTAL REDWOOD & SIERRA REDWOOD – Height versus girth: flat yew-like leaves versus wimpy asparagus.

DAWN REDWOOD – In summer, a **one-legged yew in orange flares**. In winter, a dead yew.

SCOTS PINE – Dashing, mostly **bald roué** with a salmon stuck in its branches. Thick blue-grey needles in pairs.

UMBRELLA PINE – Looks like a parasol. Long, stiff needles in pairs.

AUSTRIAN PINE – Dark, resinous-plated bark. Thick and upright. Needles in pairs.

CORSICAN PINE – Unassuming forestry tree. Slender and upright.Grey plated bark. Long needles in pairs.

MONTEREY PINE – Big trunk or several stems or short bole. Brown and orange bark in heavy plates. Long, soft needles in threes.

David Douglas and his Scottie dog

The son of a stonemason, David Douglas was born at Scone in 1799. An assiduous self-improver, he rose rapidly from apprentice gardener at Scone Palace to plant collector for the Horticultural Society. He was just 24 years old when he made his first trip to north-east America, but the awesome mountains, ravines and forests of the Pacific North-West were to become his favourite hunting ground. Over the next eleven years his tree introductions alone included the Douglas fir, Sitka spruce, Monterey pine, Pacific silver fir, noble fir, grand fir, sugar pine, digger pine, bigleaf maple and Pacific madrone (a large relative of the strawberry tree).

By 1828 he was being lionised in London, but he was a shy man, awkward and poor-sighted, infinitely more comfortable eating dried fish with Indians than doing the rounds of patrons. He responded to the overtures of polite society by wearing his dirtiest clothes and being miserably surly. In 1829 he left London, with great relief, for his longest and last trip, taking with him a Scottish terrier he named Billy. The dog was to be his

Douglas fir, introduced to Britain by David Douglas, who was ever accompanied by his Scottie dog Billy.

constant companion until his death.

Tramping alongside Douglas, Billy travelled from Hawaii to New Caledonia and California and back again. Douglas could never stay still, even in conditions that terrified others. Increasingly rheumatic, racked by fevers, his eyes burned by the glare from sun and snow, the wafer-thin Scotsman in his purple eyeglasses with his bundle on his back and his terrier at his side, criss-crossed the Pacific coast and interior for five years. Others might have been murdered, but he got on well with most of the natives (though Billy did chase their cats) and the greatest dangers were starvation and the hostile environment. In 1833, after an aborted attempt to mount an expedition to Siberia, Douglas's canoe overturned in rapids on the Fraser River and Douglas was swept far downstream through the whirlpools. Both he and Billy pulled themselves out.

By January 1834 Douglas and Billy were back in Hawaii, where they climbed three volcanoes: Mauna Kea (13,796 foot), Mauna Loa (13,678 foot) and Kilauea (4,000 foot): Douglas carried his own pack and instruments, weighing 60lb. His feet were scorched and his eyes discharging blood. In April, he set off from Honolulu on a return trip to Kilkauea with a chaplain from a seaman's mission, but his companion dropped out and Douglas and Billy continued alone. They spent the night of July 12 at the home of a cattle trapper called Ned Gurney. The next day, around noon, Douglas was found dead by natives, lying in one of Gurney's trap-pits, apparently gored by a wild bull that had fallen in. On the path, guarding his pack, sat Billy.

It looked like a horrible accident – Douglas was by then blind in his right eye and all but blind in the left – but Gurney had come from Britain via a convict's sentence in Australia and there were rumours that money was missing from Douglas's pack. The natives thought Gurney guilty, but there was no evidence against him. All Douglas left was a pathetic bundle of worn effects and some priceless journals.

He was buried on Honolulu. The grave site is now lost, but in 1934 the locals raised a monument on the slopes of Mauna Kea. And what became of Billy, his old friend, sometimes his only friend, whom Douglas had promised a pension of "four pence worth of cat's-meat per day"? It seems that he found a home with a sympathetic Foreign Office official. Perhaps he lived to enjoy some good sniffs around the Foreign Office in St James's Park, and chased a few Canada geese for old times' sake.

Revision quiz III

1. The mulberry can be encouraged to grow quickly by
a) Feeding it blood
b) Propagating it from truncheons
c) Beating it with a truncheon

2. The Judas tree
a) Will fall on your head
b) Will destroy your house
c) Will flower on its bark

3. In winter, a horse chestnut may look
a) Lupine
b) Leonine
c) Elephantine

4. The drawback with box is that it
a) Suffers from blight
b) Is associated with popery
c) Is only semi-evergreen

5. The most poisonous part of a yew is
a) The berry
b) The foliage
c) The shade

6. Since 1963, how many children in Britain have died from yew poisoning?
a) Three
b) 11,197
c) None

7. How long does a yew live?
a) 1,000 years
b) 3,000 years
c) We just don't know

8. The white poplar is
a) A big tree with white diamond-kissed bark
b) A rare black tree with a gnarled bole

c) An East London
skinhead collective

9. **The sierra redwood is
also known as**
a) The Sasquatch
b) The *Sequoia sempervirens*
c) The Wellingtonia

10. **The common lime has**
a) Red twigs
b) White candles
c) Mangy fruit

11. **Sweet chestnut bark
can look**
a) Horizontally cracked
b) Diagonally flayed
c) Vertically baked

12. **Untidy sprouting on
the base and in the
canopy might indicate a**
a) Common lime
b) Sycamore
c) Lawson cypress

13. **Which of these pines
has brilliant green foliage?**
a) Scots
c) Corsican
c) Monterey

14. **In general:**
a) The foliage of the cedar of
Lebanon is in level planes,
the Atlas ascends and the
Deodar droops
b) The Lebanon ascends, the
Atlas is level and the Deodar
droops
c) The Deodar ascends, the
Lebanon droops and the
Atlas is level

15. The **Scots pine**
a) Is the national symbol of
Scotland
b) Has salmon-pink bark
c) Was discovered by Alex
Salmond

16. **David Douglas had a
Scottie dog called**

a) Parker
b) Billy
c) Barney

17. The tallest recorded Douglas fir was
a) 120ft
b) 265ft
c) 415ft

18. How would you blet your medlar?
a) Let it rot
b) Let it be
c) Let it bleed

19. Which statement is true?
a) *Sequoia sempervirens* has foliage like wimpy asparagus. *Sequoiadendrom giganteum* has foliage like the yew
b) The coast redwood has grey bark: sierra redwood has red bark

c) The coast redwood has leaves like yew: the dawn Redwood is deciduous

20. Which of these is an autumn beauty with a flared bottom?
a) Dawn Porter
b) Dawn French
c) Dawn redwood

8. Strangers on the Street

Driving back into town and snarled up in traffic, we can sit like little gods on the top of a flyover looking out over the urban landscape. After all the grass and fields and trees it looks as if we are entering a wild, bleak land of brick foothills, concrete cliffs and glass peaks, surely too challenging a world for most trees. But many species of tree are naturally remarkably tough, while we have bred others that are still tougher, or introduced weird and wonderful species that enjoy the unusual challenges of city life and can live off a trickle of water and a whole lot of soot. So, if you look out over the city you will see, even at this leafless time of year, that the skyline is clustered with trees, singly or in regimented lines, even in small woods.

A city may be in effect a sprawling forest. In Greater London there are estimated to be some six million trees, including 65,000 woods or stands of trees. As in other forests, the "urban forest" has a canopy and an underwood, dominant trees and those that live in the shade. But the big difference between town and country is that trees are in the city largely for the work: they are rarely tolerated if they simply hang around in clumps attracting muggers, fly-tippers and dogging parties. They are expected to have a function, to do a job, and the most pressing task is to improve the surroundings for human colonisation, to be bold pioneers and transform the bleakest roads into attractive boulevards where everyone will want to live or open a shop.

The gradual change from country to city began some miles back, as the roadside woods and informal stands of oaks and ash gave way to a line of beeches planted many years ago when this was a narrow, muddy road. Then we passed modern screens of poplars, rigid as telegraph poles, shielding industrial estates and afterwards walls of evergreen cypresses alongside a sports ground, planted to prevent the wind interfering with ball games. Now, from where we sit on the flyover, we can see the first sprawling council estates and rows of horse chestnuts, marking the perimeters of parks and playgrounds, giving the residents some shade under which to sit with their prams and cans in high summer. The children can have some free cheer from the flowers and conkers, though the local authority is currently taking legal advice on whether it is liable if a child chokes on a conker or loses an eye playing conkers, and if so, should the trees be removed?

In urban areas, the familiar white horse chestnuts have often been planted in repeating patterns with red horse chestnuts, the trees with red or pinkish candles. Set against the dark leaves, the regularly spaced red candles have the look of old-fashioned wallpaper, one of those sombre red and green floral designs that you might find when stripping the wallpaper off in an old bathroom. There is something obviously pleasing about red horse chestnuts – the kind of satisfaction you get from seeing what is pretty but familiar given a new twist. Many horticultural writers dislike this tree because it has no autumn colour and it breaks easily. But the flowers do last several weeks and the tree continues to give good shade after they have vanished, so it does a job in a city. The best red is probably the popular variety called "Briotii".

The red horse chestnut is a cross between the regular horse chestnut and the red buckeye, which is itself a manageably small tree with red candles and excellent autumn colouring. Buckeye is toxic and so is the red horse chestnut, though I have not come across a case of poisoning specific to these. But the possibility of a claim for chestnut poisoning is doubtless yet another thing a local authority must consider these days. As we have seen, this is all in the mind. Trees are so rarely dangerous. But jobs must be found for some people.

In winter the red horse chestnut looks much the same as the regular white model, but it is a smaller tree growing to just 60 foot, and its widespread branches do not have the same parabolic grace as the regular horse chestnut. Its

small conkers produce inconsistent offspring and so it is often propagated by grafting. The joint may show on the bottom of its trunk – one way to distinguish it from its bigger parent when out of leaf.

The traffic moves on at last, and we move further into residential areas, some of them mean streets for tough shade trees, which must expect to take a thrashing on a Friday or Saturday night and cannot be an expensive investment for the council. Few come tougher or cheaper than the sycamore and its many variations. Purple sycamores are common and sometimes the pale, variegated "Brilliantissimum" is planted to liven things up. It is famous for its spring tinge of "shrimp pink" and is also a favourite in city gardens, but the spring colouring can have a hint of botulism and the leaves are prone to become diseased and discoloured.

Better-looking and now more frequently planted in cities than the sycamores are its northern relations, the super-hardy Norway maples. They come in a range of foliage colours from yellow to purple. Their leaves have the same basic shape as those of the sycamore, but while sycamore leaves are ragged at their edges, Norway maples have curved little horns and look like the profile of Batman with his cape raised. They also have attractively patterned

The common lime suckers and shoots with hybrid vigour, splitting concrete and tarmac

trunks on which the raised ridges of brown bark converge to form irregular diamond patterns.

Further into town the trees increase in age with the housing and soon we are moving into the territory of those traditional shade trees, the common lime and the London plane. The lime has its problems as an urban tree and perhaps ought never to have been planted in such numbers, but in the late nineteenth century, when new wealth created Pooter-villes of semi-detached villas, an avenue of limes was a final flourish, announcing that the middle-class had arrived and was cheekily stealing the symbols of those the next stage up the ladder.

Common limes resist pollution and can be mercilessly lopped to create cruelly elegant rows of pollards, each extending two fingers at its opposite number. When young, they can be contained into a convenient spade shape. Unfortunately, some of these hybrids have such a bastard vigour that cutting their tops back stimulates fierce growth. They rumble underground with fury at the abuse they suffer, sucker here and there and erupt around the base into clusters of brilliant red shoots. Swelling with frustrated energy, they lift sections of tarmac and pavement, as if they are about to up sticks and march in a mass out of town.

Forget the pavements and roads – which are after all someone else's business – the reason most people dislike limes is because they drip honeydew on the car. You know the situation: expensive car, pretty car: like to keep it in sight and peek out of the bedroom window at it, just like in the adverts. But the spot outside the house is overshadowed by a lime, and all summer long honeydew settles on the car in sugary patches which are then baked by the sun and grow sooty mould. When you wash the honeydew off it leaves rings on the paintwork: park the car in the same place and it starts all over again. The honeydew is not some spontaneous eruption of the tree. The lime aphid *Eucallipterus tilae* extracts sugar-rich sap from the tree. What the aphids cannot use they excrete. The problem varies depending on the breeding conditions for aphids. Hot dry summers will be worst. There is no solution, as it is impractical to spray a lime tree with insecticide and despite its nuisance value, most mature limes will be legally protected. The best solution is to ensure the canopy of the tree is kept small, or put a cover over the car, or buy a bicycle. It may be some small consolation to know that your local limes are intriguing ecological territory. Aphids attract ladybirds, hoverflies and butterflies. Ants are fond of aphids and protect them in return for honeydew. Aphids themselves are fascinating, since they reproduce asexually, with the females producing genetically identical offspring. Two generations are carried simultaneously inside the mother – a nymph which in turn has an embryo. Each aphid mother therefore carries her own grandchildren. Common limes, as discussed earlier, are clones. So here we have a clone inside a clone inside a clone and living on a clone. It makes humans seem the unnatural ones. It is all happening on a lime tree near you.

To be fair, limes are not always bad in cities. Given grass under them rather than streets and cars, they offer lazy shade on a summer's day. And not all city limes are the same. The Crimean lime is a clean, well-behaved tree and the Silver lime is a pretty tree with dark matt-green leaves that are silvery blue underneath. In high summer, when the cream-coloured and honey-scented flowers are out, it may be tempting to doze under the silver lime. Be careful. The nectar of the silver lime contains a potent narcotic and the ground underneath is often covered with drugged and dying bees.

When you see big London planes, you know you are coming close to the old heart of a city. The planting of the London plane as a shade tree dates back to the eighteenth century, and some of the oldest and biggest are in London's West End, in Berkeley Square. It is the most loved and effective of big city trees and is tough as old boots, able to resist pollution, impacted soil, drought and disturbance.

The outstanding feature of the London plane is its bark, which flakes off in great plates that have a camouflaged

The London plane: the great negotiator among the discordant spaces of cities.

pattern of damp green plaster and limewash. (The look is not always so distinct: sometimes the camouflage is only patchy and the thick trunks of old trees have instead a molten look to them, like the stub of a candle covered in flowing wax.) The camouflage pattern defers to its surroundings and the London plane is a great negotiator between conflicting styles of building. Take away the cream-and-green, tower-and-fountain planes and you would expose the architectural incongruities in some of London's most seductive squares. There would be fewer intimate gardens in city centres, or public spaces screened from overlooking windows. There would be an immense amount of emptiness that would bring us uncomfortably close to each other. London would look bleakly totalitarian.

On this wintry afternoon the cream patches on the planes' bark catch what is left of the daylight. And they have spiked balls of seeds, dangling like bunches of pom-poms, hard and black against the darkening sky. Some of the trees have been pollarded into stark sculptures, like huge desert cacti or hands, with swollen stumps for fingers.

We are so fond of the London plane that we are prepared to put up with the inconvenience of its seed balls, which are a serious business for asthmatics. The seed balls fall and burst apart in spring, and in dry weather the air is filled with woolly seeds that come to rest on the roads and are chucked up by passing cars. The dry spring of 2007 was particularly bad, and hospitals were busy when the seeds fell. The new leaves are also covered in fine fluff that can cause reactions. Other trees would not get off so lightly.

There is much disagreement about the origins of the London plane. It seems to be a hybrid between the oriental and occidental Planes, a compromise between East and West. One long-standing theory is that the tree originated in the Oxford Botanic Gardens around 1666, where both parents were supposed to have been present: another theory has it emerging around 1640 in the Lambeth garden founded by the Tradescant plant-hunters, father and son, but the occidental plane has never cared to mate in our climate and it seems more likely that the London plane was brought in from Spain. Many of the trees in London are genetically related clones, which would account for the similarity of forms between groups of trees planted together.

There's a serious contradiction in our relationship with trees in cities, though. In theory everybody appreciates them: even if they have little interest in nature, they understand that trees do a multitude of useful tasks. Trees mitigate the extremities of climate, which are often exaggerated in built-up areas that channel wind or reflect the sun's heat. Trees cool our homes in summer and shelter them in winter. They soften the landscape and ease tempers. They add substantially, so it is claimed, to property values.

So why are the old shade trees under threat? If you believe what you read, there is a massacre of large shade trees going on throughout the cities of Britain. Thinking about it, as we have come into town there *has* been the odd gap in, say, a line of limes or planes: nothing too drastic, just a hole here or there, where nothing else has been planted, or some incongruous little tree has been set, something short and scarcely noticeable.

It is widely rumoured that the derided "lollipop" trees – the little fruit and blossom trees of the urban underwood – are on the march, and are coming to claim the city for their own. One day there will be no more plane trees or limes or even maples, no more saturnine shade, just the cheesy grin of tediously cheerful little lollipops.

The problem is by and large money, or rather the problem is that we fear that trees will cost us money. Our houses are in many cases our savings, our pensions, our everything, and if they are threatened with subsidence caused by tree roots, we will go to our insurers who will go to the local authority who will consider all the options and then remove the problem tree and replace it – if they bother – with a token lollipop.

We should not blame local authorities. We are the hypocrites here. Most of us can probably remember a time when a little bit of subsidence was shrugged off as part of the consequence of living in a nice, tree-lined area, but our overvalued houses leave us no room for sentiment. The same people that will weep to see a tree removed from the end of their street will quickly shed their sympathies if they believe that their own house is under threat from tree roots.

Matters have been made worse by the improved drainage of urban areas. Big trees are very thirsty. A tree 50 foot high might consume around 9,000 gallons of water a year or 25 gallons a day. This presents no problem provided a tree can use its surface root system to exploit our hitherto generous annual rainfall of around 2 foot. However, if you concrete around the tree or place it in an area covered with houses and tarmac, where the rain runs off into sewers, it will have to search further and deeper for water and it may begin to dry out clay soils. Many expensive houses in south-east England sit on clay.

This is a problem with – literally – Victorian roots. Many of the larger trees in our cities were, of course, planted at the same time the houses were built, a hundred years ago or more. In those days, the future effect of tree roots was not given much thought. But, as these Victorian trees are now reaching maturity, so the problem is coming sharply into focus.

Pruning the canopy or the roots or both may hold back a tree's expansion. Walls can be built to divert roots and in most cases the roots will not be a problem. But many trees will perish by the chainsaw. What do we do? Will we be able to plant any big trees at all? Will we have to use lollipops? What are these dreaded lollipops?

Let us see if we can find a lollipop or two. They are not obvious because smaller city trees make little impression in the winter. You can see them here and there, against the window of the shops we pass, but they are like lights that are really only switched on from spring through until autumn.

Some have clear shapes if you look closely, however. Among the most easily recognizable is the Chanticleer pear. This is a tightly conical spire on a tall slender stem. In very early spring before its leaves are out it is a mass of white blossom and looks like a floral arrangement hung on a pole. The leaves linger after turning an embarrassed red in autumn and the fruits are pears proportioned for a dolls' house.

It is quite easy to muddle the Chanticleer pear with the Italian alder, one of the trees we saw in the lay-by at the beginning of our walk, which is being increasingly planted in urban areas.

At a quick glance the leaves look similar – glossy green and heart-shaped – and the Italian alder is a spire. But the trunk of the alder quickly grows thick and then leans, and then there all those dangly wotsits. And you remember the hazel in the lay-by? The one that could not remember whether it was a bush or a tree? It has an exotic cousin, the Turkish hazel, often used in towns, which shares the same sort of floppy leaves but is certain that it wants to be a tree and an attractive cone-shaped one at that.

Many of the smaller trees are rowans. The rowan is a native of English moors and Scottish mountains but copes well with town shopping centres. Not much happens where it comes from, so standing around all day and smiling at people is no problem. This is no lollipop either, though it does not always look its best in town. Great effort has gone into packing its open shape into pillar-like cultivars that will fit into nooks and crannies. These cultivars tend to crush together the profuse creamy flower heads of the tree so it looks as if it is gasping for breath. The rowan's foliage reflects its common name of mountain ash – it has feathery stalks with opposite little leaflets. Its berries are mostly red, though some imports have yellow or pale pink fruit. There is an old belief that rowans keep away witches, and this superstition must still be common for I have seen it included in the catalogues of hard-nosed commercial suppliers to the amenity business, as if witch-repellent was something councils looked for.

In urban landscapes, you sometimes find rowans planted together with a silver birch or two in a whimsical evocation of a wild landscape that cannot negate the glittering glass façade of the car dealerships or bank behind it. Birch is often used on streets by itself, but few trees look more unhappy than a solitary, pavement-bound silver birch, its bark tarnished and wounded. You might as well plant a bit of painted wood. Landscape designers accentuate the bark

Trees v buildings

The following table is included for those who like a frisson of horror. The figures in the left-hand column are taken from a survey by The Royal Botanic Gardens, Kew in the late 1970s (Cutler & Richardson, 1981) and show the maximum distance from a tree at which root damage was found. The figures on the right are the planting distances from a property recommended by the insurers Direct Line. The distances are given in feet. You can see that in practice, insurers are quite generous.

Tree	Kew (ft)	Insurers (ft)
Willow	131	59
Oak	98	59
Poplar	98	62
Elm	82	49
Horse chestnut	75	32
Ash	69	49
Lime	66	26
Maple/sycamore	66	29
Plane	49	26
Beech	49	29
Black locust	39	26
Hawthorn	39	23
Rowans etc	36	23

colour by planting the tree in clusters in oversized pots, or by using the Himalayan birch, *jaquemontii*, which in theory has pure white, peeling bark. The peeling coloured bark of other exotic birch species also makes them attractive features but only in the more privileged areas of a city. Not all of them are tough and the bark is an irresistible temptation to fiddling fingers.

Our public parks often have little groves of round-topped trees that look like mushrooms, or monopods moving on crooked knees. These are probably hawthorns or crab apples. Hawthorns have long been used in urban planting and old parks may contain old trees the names of which are long lost: you may find twisted antique beauties like the medlar-hawhorn hybrid. The most common hawthorn cultivar is probably, Paul's Scarlet. It does not have scent or fruits but its double, rose-pink blossoms lend a rustic, cottage-garden air to its surroundings.

Other commonly used thorns include the broad-leafed cockspur thorn and Lavellei's thorn. The former is a low, rounded tree with jauntily upright branches when young purple new twigs, big, bold red fruit and strong red and gold autumn colours. It is a sharp little tree, with fierce spines: a romantic, but also sternly didactic when necessary. It is often found lurking in park flower beds, waiting to smack the hands of mean-spirited children. Lavellei's thorn is a shapely little tree with glossy green oval leaves that linger into winter and large waxy orange fruit.

A popular cultivar "Carrierei" puts a classy, polished sheen on exposed road-sides. The blossom is a bit stinky.

Crab apples are an essential part of the urban under-wood, though these days their suitability has inevitably been questioned both in play areas (children may eat the fruit and get stomach aches) and pedestrian areas (shop-pers may slip on the ripe fruit and fall over). But we need our crab apples in cities, just as much as we need maples or planes. They have masses of pink-and-white blossom and can grow in heavy cold soils that dismay Japanese cherries – and the birds love the fruit. Some of the best in parks and gardens are Golden Hornet (exceptionally fruity, lots of little yellow apples), Red Sentinel (excep-tionally tight-fisted, hanging onto its red fruit all winter) and John Downie (extremely tasty, slightly larger crab apples, and a good pollinator of other trees). The pillar apple is a peculiarly upright tree, with very steeply ascend-ing side branches that resist contact with the world below and give it a snooty look. It is very useful along roadside verges. It has pink blossom, small round yellow-purple fruits and pleasant autumn russets.

These trees scarcely seem offensive and their shapes are too varied to be dismissed as lollipops. Some will grow big given the chance. Perhaps the lollipop-phobes are thinking of those favourite trees of the arterial ring-road, the Swedish whitebeam and the so-called bastard service tree.

The Swedish whitebeam is a roughly rounded, small tree, with sallow greenish bark on its smooth, clean trunk. It has glossy leaves reminiscent of an oak, toothily serrated but more pointed. The cluster of white flowers yield red berries. The machined, fastidious look of this northern European tree – more like an item of furniture than a tree – is deceptive. This is an immensely tough and versatile character. It has been much planted where there are extreme, exposed conditions along busy roadsides or in windswept new developments, but it has also spread to residential streets and squares, everywhere an all-purpose, decorative yet unassertive tree is required. It does an excellent job, but its clean, functional features can be monotonous and look pragmatic when it is planted in large numbers or near irregular, old buildings. It seems to make a place look cold. (This is one of the few trees that will grow up in the Orkneys.)

It is, however, nowhere near as conspicuously tidy as the bastard service tree, a cross between the whitebeam and the rowan with a canopy so smoothly rounded the tree appears to be wrapped in cling film. Even in the nude it looks so neatly circular you might assume that the council came round at night and shaped it with a hedge-cutter. The bastard service tree has an air of obsessive insecurity: it simply must prove itself useful. It is often put to work overseeing large supermarket car parks where it will cast some shade but will also guarantee a clear space below the branches for cars to park. It remains psychotically tense when taken off car park duty and is quite out of place among period houses. Its leaves are similar to those of the Swedish whitebeam but break apart at the base into separate small lobes, like the hilt of a knife, as if the tree were disintegrating into a psychotic state.

Whitebeams are not generally so tense as the above duo, remaining nicely proportioned and mostly beautiful to see on the street. We have a native whitebeam that grows shrub-like in chalky areas of Britain. More organised versions light up our cities with pale, velvet-green spring foliage that gives the trees a magical silver appearance – the breaking buds can be mistaken for the flowers of a magnolia. Some whitebeam cultivars – "Mitchell" especially – have enormous, felted leaves, big as ears and almost white underneath,

I would hate to say that a whitebeam could be boring, but you can have too much of a good thing and it is possible to have a tyranny of soft silvery foliage among dusty grey concrete. It begins to look like mould or as if you are an insect in a herb garden, and you become conscious that the problem with smaller trees is that you are confronted all the time with their leaves. They are not above you, but in your face.

Still, I have a lot of affection for the city underwood trees, even the bastard lollipop. I feel sorry for them. These are performers for whom the show never stops, year in year out, and they are also supposed to be tidy, upright and youthful model citizens. Here are one northern council's wistful rules on street trees.

A street tree:

1. Should not cause damage.
2. Should be upright in nature.
3. Should establish quickly and easily
4. Should be robust, healthy and not prone to disease
5. Should be easily maintained (trunk to be 2.5m clear above pavement, 5m clear above carriage ways)
6. Should not drop branches
7. Should not have fruit with an unpleasant odour

The little trees must stand as an example to the crooked, sick, irresponsible, high-maintenance people. Be more like a tree, and when life cocks its leg on you, just smile. One would have to be a true pessimist to see the little trees supplanting the shade trees. There would be an uproar – as there is now, even at the rumour of such a revolution. We like our city trees to have a sylvan romance, and for all their colour and tricks, there is something too human and too frail about the smaller trees. They are just as threatened by litigation or by environmental changes as the big trees and many are subject to diseases. It is a sad fact that small city trees have short lives. It tends to be a matter of live fast, die young, stay a lollipop. Or a column, or a cone.

We are sure to lose many of the big Victorian trees, but the trick will be to allow in future planning for trees to grow alongside new buildings and to find species that can deal with the changed circumstances – basically, that can survive drought. Climate change may bring another wave of interesting new trees to our streets, imports just like the horse chestnut, common lime and plane once were. It should be an exciting prospect, not depressing.

One drought-resistant large tree already planted in numbers is the black locust or *Robinia pseudoacacia*, a tall, gaunt North American import with black corky bark. This is an outsized mixture of rose and pea, sometimes having brutal thorns as well as sparse pea-like tresses of leaves, dripping threads of white, vanilla-scented flowers and dangling seed pods. The leaves go floppy at night, giving the impression that the tree is sleeping.

The popularity of *Robinia* seems at first to be a mystery. Its foliage has often been derided as rubbish: it comes out late and drops early. During the summer the tree offers poor shade that does not cool (it has a low transpiration rate to save water) and in the winter it can look about as welcoming as a thin and swarthy tramp standing in the shadows. It also has a reputation for sending out roots and suckers that endanger neighbouring buildings and is said to be dangerously brittle.

However, to know this tree is to appreciate it. Not only is it drought-resistant, but it has an impressive photosynthetic ability, which means – if you are at all climate-minded – it can absorb lots of CO_2 with very few leaves. Nor do I mind its shape. Look at some of the places where it is planted, right up against tall blocks of flats – what other big tree could be squeezed in there and break up those miserable façades without spreading out and causing problems? The roots of black locust are not so questing as those of the plane or lime and tree surgeons say that so far as the suckering goes, there is a problem only when you cut the tree down and it tries to regenerate. You try to get rid of me, I make big problem. As for its brittleness, I have read that it grows strongest in the poorest conditions, for then it grows slowly. So starve it to be safe.

Several cultivars are used in cities, particularly "Bessoniana", a compact thornless version, and "Frisia", which has pale yellow foliage. Some confusion arises with the honey locust, or gleditsia. This is smaller but better armed than black locust – nasty, long spines – though the most-used cultivar is the thornless, gold-leafed "Sunburst", which was bred in 1953 and has become a ubiquitous suburban planting. A little Sunburst lights up the road but too much and its airy, perfect yellow is like a relentless smile. You might be at a rally in North Korea.

There are many other trees already growing in our

parks that could be used on our streets. We will have a look for some of them before we make it home. But now let us consider something we have in common with the Japanese: our love of flowering cherries.

Bare essentials

LONDON PLANE – **military camouflaged bark**, dangling clusters of pom-pom seed heads.

COMMON LIME (in city) – Ferocious suckering. Lifting pavements. Red growth. **Aphids**. Silver lime & Crimean lime are cleaner trees without suckering. The former has blue-silver underside to leaves and lots of stoned bees in summer.

ROBINIA (black locust) – Fissured, dark bark. Tall, gaunt stems. **Dangling dried pea-pods.** Pea-like foliage, pale yellow on "Frisia", vanilla-scented white flowers.

GLEDITSIA "SUNBURST" – Evokes rows of cheerfully smiling people saluting the Glorious Leader. Otherwise, similar to Robinia "Frisia" but thornless.

SYCAMORE **"BRILLIANTISSIMUM"** – Shrimp pink, or **regurgitated prawn cocktail** in spring.

MAPLES – Dense, upswept branches with opposite twigs giving look of ship's rigging. Brown, attractively ridged bark.

Lollipop guide

SPIRES AND CONES – Chanticleer pear, pillar apple, Italian alder, Turkish hazel.

PILLARS AND BOLLARDS – rowan cultivars.

MUSHROOMS AND MONOPODS – hawthorns and crab apples.

BALLS ON STICKS – Swedish whitebeam and Bastard Service Tree

The black locust scam

The *Robinia pseudoacacia* was at the centre of an oft-related tree-swindle perpetrated by the unlikely figure of the radical rural reformer William Cobbett. The tree was a native of the Appalachians, where it was described by William Strachey in 1610 as "a kind of low tree, which beares a cod like unto the peas". Known as "locust", it was later planted in New England, where Cobbett spent the years 1817-19 managing a farm. Cobbett had to leave America in a hurry after he accused George Washington's physician of having killed the President. He returned to England with a huge quantity of *Robinia* seed – and the body of Thomas Paine, author of the Rights of Man, whom Cobbett had disinterred and vowed to bury under a grand monument in England.

In London Cobbett announced that he had discovered the "tree of trees" out of which the Navy would build its future ships. In 1823 he set up his own nursery in West London and, using his considerable public profile, sold a million seedlings. Forests of *Robinia pseudoacacia* sprung up across Britain. The speculators lost heavily. Cobbett's seed produced poor trees which were in any case soon made redundant by the use of steel in ships.

Contemporary plantsmen observed that commercially planted Robinia was very susceptible to wind damage when young, but it is possible that the trees were also spoiled by good soil. (As previously described, it is known that *Robinia* produces its best wood when it grows slowly under nutritionally impoverished circumstances.)

The species had long since been introduced and planted in Britain where it was known as the "bastard" or "false" acacia. Cobbett falsely claimed his imported tree was something quite different: he marketed his trees under the American name of locust, and charged six times the going rate.

The idea of the black locust being grown for ship's timber was not in fact so strange: the wood can be strong and is resistant to decay. In America, it had been used for "treenails" – wooden pins that would swell when damp, holding the boat's structure together. There had been wide enthusiasm for the black locust in New England during Cobbett's time, but the tree proved susceptible to an insect borer.

Despite Cobbett's profits, Thomas Paine never had his memorial. After Cobbett's death in 1835, the coffin of Paine was sold at auction to a furniture dealer and Paine's body disappeared.

9. Cherry Blossom Comrades

After reaching the city centre we turn south, back into more residential areas where the plane trees recede and the limes return, and sometimes, outside houses with a half-timbered 1930s look, there are rows of cherries, their glossy ruby bark glowing with reflected light. If you look into the front gardens we are passing there are lots more cherries, of different shapes and sizes. Some have long branches, some weep, others yearn upwards, leaving an impression of bronze hieroglyphics scribbled on the dark page of the winter's afternoon. Some trees still cling to long tear-shaped leaves that have turned scarlet. But we are not much interested in the bark or foliage of cherries. We plant them for their spring blossom.

The appreciation of cherry blossom or *sakura* is a national ritual in Japan. In early spring the *sakura zensen* or cherry blossom front rolls north over the Japanese islands. Celebrations are planned: the Japanese enjoy *sakuragari* (cherry blossom hunting up in the mountains); *yozakura* (looking for cherry blossom after dark); *hanamizake* (drinking sake while viewing cherry blossoms); and *hana-mi* (picnicking and singing under cherry blossoms).

While these would mostly be impractical in a British spring, our cities are indebted to the cherries that scatter pink confetti over our gridlocked cars or froth gently like bubble bath at the foot of high rise flats. Throughout the darkest months we also enjoy the calming presence of the winter flowering cherry *Prunus subhirtella* x *autumnalis*, a slender tree with a few quickly sketched boughs and simple pale white and pink blossom. In the shelter of city gardens it flowers quietly from November onwards, reaching a muted crescendo in early spring. But it is really too polite a tree for us.

Most of our favourite Japanese cherries are *satozakura*, or temple cherries, the product of hundreds of years of cultivation. They are typically low and spreading. In the earliest flowering cherries, the blossoms often appear on naked twigs, emphasising their transient beauty. Few of the trees have fruit: most are grafted. This is a pure, sexless aesthetic.

The basic form of a Japanese flowering cherry is a large "Y", with one of the principal limbs slightly dominant: using this shape, the monks and gardeners of Japan bred trees that evoked wind and water and moons and mountains. In Japan they may be reverentially tended, ancient trees but their life on British streets is short and testing. The low, spreading cloud shape of a Shirofugen ends up like the head of a scrubbing brush: the weeping limbs of a *Shogetsu* resemble a drowned bathroom spider.

Too bad about the shape. All we Brits want is blossom, lots of blossom. We always want more for our money. More chocolate, more chips, more blossom. The Japanese are careful about the use of deep pink blossom— not too much of it among the white, preferably pale and restrained – but what do they know? We love deep, deep pink cherry blossom: on streets and in gardens, front lawns, hedgerows, terraces and pots. Even the terrifying bald guy down the road with the beer gut and braces and the bull terrier loves a pink cherry.

We love the clotted-pink, supplicating boughs of a Cheal's weeping. Better yet, we love the Kanzan. In Japan the low-branching funnel shape of the Kanzan is a carefully employed flower vase, but to us it looks like a huge ice-cream cone waiting to be filled with a strawberry Mr Whippy topped with jam. Its double pink flowers have as many as 50 petals: the superfluity is irresistible to our brains. The frilly flowers are like something optimistically purchased for the missus from Ann Summers. With age, the branches arch out and the Kanzan collapses into an ugly tangle but what do we care so long as it stays pink?

Kanzan is sometimes planted in roadside displays alternating with Ukon, a similar spreading ice cream cone of semi-double green-yellow flowers. The effect is a French nougat pattern of old Y-fronts and pink knickers; but per-

haps the acidic harshness of the built world can only be
neutralised by what is most naturally, profusely sweet and
vulgar.

Cherries of all sorts have glossy grey and red bark with
multiple bands round their trunks as if they had removed a
score of wedding rings. Many Japanese cherries have identical boles because they are grafted onto stems of our
native wild cherry or gean. In time the gean, its heart in
our woodlands, becomes oppressed by its Japanese other
half, who yearns for mountains and shrines. The gean
grows cross and stout. The fractured Anglo-Japanese relationship shows as a swelling graft but even with this wound
the marriage plods on for many years.

On its own, the gean sings the arrival of spring every bit
as loud as the Japanese cherries. It is a native of our woods
and it is planted commercially for timber. Not to be confused with the shrubby, sour-scented bird cherry, an old
Gean can be a 90-foot, billowing spire of white blossom
around Easter-time. Such a combination of size and delica-
cy is not plausible in the British spring. No, no: it is a
mirage. The roving eye moves on, as if it had seen and dismissed the sight of an immense white elephant dancing on
tiptoe among the naked branches of a distant wood. Must
get the eyes tested.

In the public park the gean shows a testy wildness,
suckering and setting seeds from small red fruit. It refuses
to be tidy; the symmetrical cone may decide to grow

additional stems or lean drunkenly towards the light. The bark-skin peels and the split trunks of old trees look like burned, exploded sausages.

On a warm, clear April day a big gean will draw the eye upwards to survey its slender blossom-tipped branches that cross-hatch the blue sky like leading in a high stained-glass window. It may also give you a sore neck.

The gean likes space and is not good for streets but the 300-year-old cultivar "Plena" – a smaller, spreading tree with pendulous double white flowers – is commonplace. It mixes easily with the Japanese cherries which are also mostly low and wide. (The exception being Amanagawa, an unmistakable pale-pink squashed spire). The most spectacular of the Japanese whites is the Taihaku, or great white cherry which has huge blooms like big silk flowers. It was thought to have vanished altogether in the eighteenth century, but was rediscovered in 1923, growing in a Sussex garden.

Enough of the whites. We want pink! We like pink so much that we have developed our own pinks, because the Japanese pinks were mostly not pink enough. Pinker please! Okame, an early deep pink tree small enough for most gardens, was developed in 1947 by Captain Collingwood Ingram, a man with a passion for Japanese

Pink cherries against concrete. Sometimes what is most brutal can only be countered by what is most obvious.

cherries, who introduced many of our favourites. Later, Accolade must have caused a stir when it was launched in Britain in the dour 1950s, because it is a semi-double early bird that is the first strong pink of the year. Pink Perfection has a double or semi-double flower, the product of a Surrey marriage between Kanzan and the pretty white Shogetsu which has dangling blossoms. The hanging flowers of Pink Perfection have differing pink tinges and seem to change tint as they move in the wind. Two pinks in one! And our pinks are earlier than the Japanese pinks!

Not, however, as early as the ubiquitous purple-leafed cherry-plum. A relation of our native Myrobalan plums, this is theoretically a harmonious combination of pink blossom, dark rusted bark and deep purple foliage. In practice the whole thing looks like a bad haematoma. The most common cultivar is the evocatively named "Pissardii" which is planted in countless urban front gardens, its saturnine foliage serving as a privacy screen.

Perhaps the best pink of all, and among the most impressive of flowering cherries, is Sargent's cherry, a 30-foot rounded dome of rose-pink flowers in early spring and scarlet foliage in autumn. It is a native species of Japan and Korea where it is grown for its timber, and it even has some fruit. This is a flowering cherry you can climb up into, or string a children's swing from.

We may go overboard with the pink but there is an uncomplicated pleasure in our love of flowering cherries.

In Japan, *sakura* has an occasionally melancholy connotation. Flowering cherries, and in particular the Yoshino, are reminders of a painful history. In Japan the majority of trees – some 90% – are Yoshino, which is white with the palest of pink shades. It was first bred in the town of Somei in the early nineteenth century and named after Yoshino now a suburb of Toyko once famous for its blossom. In the West, the name Yoshino, now covers a number of similar trees, some of which bear fruit. But the original Somei-Yoshino is a large, barren tree exceptional for the way its flowers open simultaneously, giving a rapturous, brief display of uniformity.

By the early 20th century, cherry blossom had become a symbol of burgeoning Japanese nationalism. The Somei-Yoshino was planted throughout public areas and in schools, where it was a living lesson to children about the glory of a short but beautiful life. In 1912 the Japanese gave 3,000 Somei-Yoshino cherries to the United States government to be planted in Washington DC. Though these were a gesture of friendship, their blossom was also a conqueror's flag. When the Japanese later occupied Taiwan and Korea, they planted countless Somei-Yoshino – trees which the locals have since removed. The Japanese language textbook issued in the occupied territories began with the words: "*Saita, saita! Sakura sa saita!*" ("They've blossomed! They've blossomed! The cherries have blossomed!") Those Washington cherries were scarcely mature when the Japanese attacked Pearl Harbour.

Later, the kamikaze squadrons were named after blossoms – the *Yamasakura-Tai* was the mountain cherry blossom corps – and their aircraft were decorated with pictures of *sakura*. Military songs reinforced the analogy.

You and I are cherry blossom comrades
Blooming in the same garden of our squadron
Knowing that cherry blossoms soon must fall
Let us fall bravely for our country...

Though we must fall one by one
Let us return to Yasukuni Shrine
And meet again
As blossoms in the same garden.

Yasukuni Shrine is the temple commemorating Japan's war dead. In recent times, the Japanese have refreshed their cherry stock by taking grafts from those trees they sent to Washington at the beginning of the last century.

Our own blossom associations are happier. For a while we see the world not through a red mist, but a white and pink cloud. It is indecent to be rude under the falling blossom. We nod to our neighbours, while the youths who usually gather like crows at twilight under the low boughs of an old cherry move down the road to frequent the leafless maples. And if we should hanker for cherry blossom with a little less sugar, we can always go at Easter to the park or woods and hunt down the improbable gean. Its brief blossoms may have intimations of mortality but they should encourage us nonetheless to stay and enjoy the scenery as long as possible.

Loveliest of trees, the cherry now
Is hung with bloom along the bough
And stands about the woodland ride
Wearing white for Eastertide.

Now, of my threescore years and ten
Twenty will not come again
And take from seventy springs a score,
It only leaves me fifty more.

And since to look at things in bloom
Fifty springs are little room,
About the woodland I will go
To see the cherry hung with snow.

AE Housman

It is possible to have a continuous display of
"Japanese" blossom from February until June. Times
of flowering vary according to locality and weather
but here is a sequence commencing in February
and ending in May.

Cherry	Shape	Colour
Winter Flowering	Wispy model	Pretty anaemic
Okame	Neat and stumpy	Varnished pink
Accolade	Insect legs	Dangling pink
Kursar	Royal hand-wave	Smokey pink
Fuji	Volcanic eruption	Pale pink
Yoshino	Graceful cloud	Dawn blush
Sargent's Cherry	Big lawn tree	Profuse pink
Shirotae	Flat cloud	Large white
Taihaku	Rumbling cloud	White roses
Cheal's Weeping	Sparsely grieving	Thickly pink
Amanagowa	Crushed commuter	Last-gasp pink
Ukon	Double scoop	Mint-vanilla
Kanzan	Double scoop	Extra strawberry
Pink Perfection	Melting scoop	Strawberry Cornetto
Shirofugen	Millennium dome	Slow sunset white to pink
Shogetsu	Courteous ghost	Dangling white with green leaves

Revision quiz IV

1. **Robina Pseudoacacia is otherwise known as**
a) Black poplar
b) Black thorn
c) Black locust

2. **Silver limes**
a) Have bark that peels off in plates
b) Produce nectar that is a narcotic to bees
c) Were discovered during the Crimean war

3. **"Briotii" is a common cultivar of**
a) The Italian alder
b) The Lombardy poplar
c) The red horse chestnut

4. **London planes have**
a) Pom-poms of seeds that dangle throughout the winter
b) Pea-pods of seeds that dangle throughout the winter
c) A reputation for dripping honey dew

5. **A compact, domed tree with candelabras of felted, silvery-green leaves, sometimes white underneath. Could this be**
a) A pillar apple
b) A whitebeam
c) A silver lime

6. **Black locust is**
a) A swarthy upright tree with pea-like foliage and seed pods
b) A spire-shaped tree with small brown fruits
c) A North American tree discovered by William Cobbett

7. **The spring phase of the sycamore "Brilliantissimum" is described as**
a) Shrimp pink
b) Salmon pink
c) Gammon pink

8. **The cleanest deciduous lollipop shape is probably**
a) The poor service tree
b) The dreadful service tree
c) The bastard service tree

9. **The name of a ubiquitous double-pink hawthorn is**
a) Will Scarlet
b) Captain Scarlet
c) Paul's Scarlet

10. **The name of a ubiquitous double pink cherry is**
a) Ukon
b) Mekon
c) Kanzan

11. Which of these common trees has the shortest root run?
a) Horse chestnut
b) Black locust
c) Willow

12. **The name of a ubiquitous purple-leaved plum is**
a) Pissardii
b) Pisseadii
c) Pissoffii

13. **"Shirofugen" is**
a) A Japanese cherry shaped like a spreading funnel
b) A Japanese cherry shaped like a spreading cloud
c) A Japanese cherry beloved by AE Housman

14. **Which Japanese cherry could you plant in a narrow space?**
a) Sargent's cherry
b) Amanogawa

c) Taihaku

15. Which popular crab apple has masses of yellow fruit?
a) Golden handshake
b) Golden showers
c) Golden hornet

16. The gean blossoms
a) Around Easter
b) In February
c) Given space

17. Jaquemontii is
a) A species of box elder
b) A Himalayan birch with white, peeling bark
c) A Canadian policeman

18. Rowans have
a) Small opposite leaflets on feathery stalks
b) Variegated foliage that tends to revert
c) Fierce spines feared by witches

19. The Japanese term for cherry blossom is
a) *Saki*
b) *Sakura*
c) *Shirotae*

20. London planes have
a) Green and cream camouflage trunks
b) Green and cream camouflage leaves
c) Green and cream camouflage pants

10. Out of the Woods

Where do you live, by the way? I mean, it would help if I knew where we were going. I want to find us a public park to have a quick look around. Home is what? That sounds interesting. Half a flat in a subdivided Victorian semi-detached house. You must earn a packet. And there is a kind of park, you say, but you rarely go into it and have no idea of what trees are there. The parks sits in the middle of the Victorian development and it had, you know, a bit of a reputation as the kind of place you went shopping for one thing or another. Certainly, it would not do to go wandering around it staring at the trees.

I know your park and I have news for you. The shocking price of property may be threatening our big shade trees, but it has had a beneficial effect on recreation spaces. Your park has been taken in hand. There is a local residents' committee, which you take no interest in, which has got historians involved and has shamed the local authority into action and wheedled some lottery money for restoration of the old tennis courts, playground, bandstand and café, and to pay for the borders to be made over and the trees to be catalogued. The park is now tidy, safe and relaxed and the most intoxicating substance you can buy there is a latte. Now, don't get sentimental for the good old bad old days. None of that "you used to be able to buy anything, now it's all nannies and babies and joggers." Save that for the dinner parties. If you want an edge on your urban life there are still many mean cities you can move to.

We reach your area at sunset. The park is a rough circle of three or four acres, set around with iron railings and big gates on opposing sides of its perimeter. You are so lucky. It is a smashing place, a huge garden for the people who live in the late Victorian villas that ring it. Places like this are what make Britain's cities so special, this common land where you can share plants and trees that it would be impossible to have in the average garden.

The park-keeper is just doing his rounds and if we leave the car on this side of the park, we could slip across and out the other side before we are locked in. That would bring us almost to your doorstep.

Inside the gates, a new tarmac path gleams like dark water. To either side stand tall trees, their tops sharp against the fading light. It is one of those blue wintry evenings that linger on in the city, extended by streetlamps casting tiger stripes of light out across the grass. It is windless. The trees are still, and dead leaves are falling gently to the grass. You can almost hear the noise they make, like a distant faint tinkling. Curious how at night some trees seem almost more noticeable than in the day, their presence magnified by shadows. They swell into giants and open into voids, as if they had another life after dark. It makes you wish you knew them better by daylight so you could dispel the feeling that you are being watched.

This last leg of our trip is a voyage down the river of the tarmac path, a trip of a just few hundred yards that will take us from Peking in old China to Hiroshima in Japan and then back across the Pacific to the Wild West of America. We have time to take in only a handful of trees from these locations, trees that you can find in public parks and sometimes, whether you like it or not, in your own garden. They can be beautiful and strange and even frightening.

First let us sail to China, in the eighteenth century regarded as the land of celestial beings and the destiny for service or exile of many Jesuits. We owe much to the Jesuits, the Roman Catholic order devoted to reconciling God and nature; but in retrospect the tree of heaven was not their finest gift to the West. It is the first tree on our right in the park, emerging furtively from a shrubbery, a tall thin thing, almost branchless, looking like a skinny moll who has fled home in a hurry, dressed only in a few oversized hairpins.

The tree should not be here: it is peering out to see if the coast is clear and planning its next move. Should it lurch rapidly skywards a few yards, or send out some suckers and replicate itself in the cover of another shrubbery? The park used to be a favourite base for the tree of heaven's operations, but there are now concerted efforts to curtail the tree's spread or move it on altogether. There is a kind of arrogance to the tree though, and even if it is attacked, it is fairly confident of survival, either by strength of guile, because it is so tough and swift-growing, and also because of its good looks. It is easy to chop down a sycamore but it is harder to take a chainsaw to a tree with such smooth and serpentine, green-tinged, wet-looking bark as the tree of heaven.

Tall and erect as its name suggests, the tree of heaven also has wonderfully elaborate foliage not dissimilar to the ash or sumach – languid, fern-like tresses, but extra-long, with up to twenty pairs of opposing leaves on each little stalk. These emerge slowly and late, with rose and ruby flushes and later the flat-pointed seed pods turn pink so the tree blushes coyly both at the beginning and end of the year. We know how much we like pink. We cannot chop down anything with a hint of pink. The branches also have endearing leaf scars like bamboo, that suggest, wrongly, an inner vulnerability.

The tree of heaven has terrifying powers of regeneration. Cut it down on one side of your garden and it will pop up suckers on the other side. Cut it down there and it will emerge in your neighbour's garden or in the middle of a nearby pavement. It seeds prolifically – a single female tree can disperse 325,000 winged pods – and will set itself in tarmac or concrete forecourts, and is able to live without food or water and still grow 10 foot a year. To make matters worse, it poisons the ground around it, secreting self-produced weed-killers – those allelopathic phytotoxins previously mentioned in connection with our cunning old friend the horse chestnut – which damage a range of common trees.

If you remain unimpressed and attack the foliage, you'll quickly find yourself gagging in a stinking miasma reminiscent of a landfill site. The stench emanates from oil glands at the base of leaves: the white male flowers are worse. In summer this malodorous body ripens quickly and on hot days this is the tree that stinks to high heaven.

Save yourself the trouble. Admit defeat. The tree of heaven is here to stay. It is mustering in shrubberies and in the corners of car parks and odd pieces of ground behind tennis courts and garages. It is already sneaking under your damp course, as voracious as Audrey in the *Little Shop of Horrors*.

And yet in the beginning it was different. In 1751, in the Chelsea Physic Garden, Philip Miller planted the first seeds of the tree of heaven that had reached Europe. His hands must have trembled with excitement to have in his possession the fruit of that magical kingdom of China! The Chinese regarded outsiders as inferior intruders, and seeds from China were treasure stolen from the land of the gods.

The seeds had been sent to Europe by Father Pierre Nicholas le Cheron d'Incarnville, from the Jesuit station in Peking. D'Incarnville was to send seeds of the pagoda tree and the golden rain tree to the West, but the tree of heaven proved his most vigorous discovery. Its resistance to drought and pollution resulted in it becoming a favourite urban planting, particularly in North America, where it is now designated an invasive weed in 44 states. In Britain it is falling out of popularity. Just as well, for if our climate warms appreciably it may become the Japanese knotweed of trees.

Time to move on. A little way off the path, standing alone in a small clearing, is a tall, clean trunk touched by street light with a tight canopy high and round against the evening sky. This is the handkerchief tree, otherwise known as the dove tree or ghost tree. Its peculiar shape, with the canopy above a clean stem and nothing in between, is not natural: it is sometimes trimmed this way so that people can stand under it and look up at the flowers. In the past, plant hunters risked everything to find these flowers. Strictly speaking they are not flowers, nor are they leaves, but bracts, that come in pairs in late spring, hanging either side of the flower to shelter it. The bracts are large, white, ragged tongues and since they are of unequal length each flower is unbalanced. The slightest breeze and the tree gets the jitters and its bracts start flapping to and fro – like a flock of agitated birds or, on a spring evening, something white and spooky doing a *danse macabre*.

In practice it is not a uniform effect: some bracts may be affected more than others, so the tree seems inhabited by numerous personalities. The wind catches one flower and the longest bract of the pair starts pumping as if it were furiously conducting an orchestra; another bract will be still, while yet another will wake up and jiggle half-heartedly before going back to sleep, while its neighbour is still gyrating rapidly. It is not a ghost so much as a ghost party.

The effect is best appreciated from directly under-neath, hence the manner in which it is trimmed. It is real-ly a one-trick pony – an invaluable piece of ornamental planting, though it may take many years to flower. It has small round fruit that might at a distance be mistaken for those of a plane tree in winter, but they hang singly and, in any case, the bark of the dove tree is orange-brown and cracked.

The dove tree, *Davidia involucrata*, was legendary in Britain long before it was grown here. Like the tree of heaven, it was brought to the attention of plant hunters by a Roman Catholic priest, Abbé Armand David, a Lazarist missionary in Peking. Abbé David had an interest in natu-ral history and was granted leave to undertake several extensive expeditions into the Chinese interior. In 1868 he embarked on a two-year trip that took him to the margins of Tibet. There he was the first Westerner to see the giant panda, a specimen of which he shipped back to Paris, where it unfortunately died. He also sent back dried specimens of the dove tree. The beauty of the tree was apparent but no seed was forthcoming, and the dove tree remained as remote as it was desirable.

Seventeen years later, Augustine Henry, a young Irish medical officer in the Imperial Chinese Maritime Customs Service, offered his services as a plant collector to the Royal Botanic Gardens at Kew. Stationed up the Yangtze at Ichang, Henry had plenty of time on his hands. His first batch of specimens was impressive and was soon venturing further afield. In 1888, he collected foliage specimens of a mysterious tree which caused great excitement at Kew when it was identified from published illustrations of David's discoveries. Henry had found the dove. Though he agreed with correspondents that "*Davidia* is worth any amount of money," he himself was not interested in the loot. He said he had seen only one tree and would not be persuaded by commercial growers to look for it again.

In 1899, shortly before Henry left China for good, he was visited by Ernest Henry Wilson, a horticultural graduate who had been dispatched by the Chelsea nursery of James Veitch & Sons with stern instructions to come back with the dove tree: "This is the object – do not dissipate time, energy or money on anything else." Wilson was just

22 years old: he had never travelled abroad before and could not speak a word of Chinese. Henry gave him a sketch map of the approximate area of the tree's location, some ten days' travel up the Yangtze – a vague treasure map that would have tested the will of the most obdurate pirate. It was a minor miracle that Wilson had found Henry. This was surely a mission impossible.

Somehow Wilson got there. Braving drowning and bandits, he located the village that Henry had visited a dozen years previously. Yes, the locals remembered Henry, and yes, they could tell Wilson where to find the tree. Wilson trotted behind them. "After about two miles," he recalled, "we came to a house rather new in appearance." Nearby was the Stump of Henry's *Davidia*. The legendary tree, the El Dorado of the nurserymen, had become a spanking des res. Wilson was distraught. Gutted, in modern parlance.

Fortunately, the story had a happy ending of sorts. Wilson did find more dove trees, and was able to send seed back. But unfortunately, he had been pipped at the post. In 1897, yet another Roman Catholic missionary, Père Paul Guillaume Farges, had sent seeds of the dove to the French plantsman Maurice de Vilmorin, one of which germinated in France in 1898. Wilson's seed produced thousands of trees, Vilmorin's just one; but the latter tree turned out to be hardier and most of the dove trees planted in Britain are the species "Vilmoriniana". Indeed the Lord giveth, and he taketh away. Wilson was to have other, easier triumphs.

A third popular introduction from China is the fox-glove tree, brought to Europe via the Dutch East Indies Company in 1830. It can grow up to 40 foot in sheltered areas and has upright spires of tubular blue or lilac flowers (from which it has its common name) and almond-shaped brown seed pods that linger on stiff twigs in winter. It is sometimes also called the empress tree because it was reputedly so beautiful that it was planted on the graves of Chinese empresses.

The Americans attempted to grow it for timber. However, it produces up to 20 million seeds per tree which are carried on the wind and quickly set themselves in disturbed ground. In the warmer parts of North America it has become a pest. In the British climate there is no such problem. It can be used as an attractive street tree and you can find it planted around sheltered squares and streets, where it tends to have a naked, slender, green-ish stem and a sparsely branched canopy like the ruins of an inside-out umbrella. On warm nights the scent seems to drop from the high-up flowers, sweet and fruity— almost like strawberries. It is not perfectly hardy, and is often cut back to a shrubby bush to stimulate production of the massive leaves.

We will be stuck in China all night unless we are care-ful. Let us hop back in the boat and sail rapidly along the path to Japan. The first Japanese introduction comes rear-ing up next to the path, a tree shaped like the fingers of a hand held up in warning, as if to say: go no further. It is too thick-limbed and straight to be a maple and its bark, if you rub it in the dark, is rough and scaling like a pan-scrubber. This is an elm known in Japan as a keaki – which means "tree that looks like an upraised hand". We also know it as the *Zelkova serrata*. In Japan it was an important timber tree and the tough but elastic wood supported the roofs of temples. At the end of summer the leaves turn orange or amber with immaculate consistency. On mature trees, the bark is also orange and in the autumn the keaki hums melodiously with tasteful muted colour. It is a superb landscape tree but little planted outside cities, though it has been here since the late nineteenth century and seems fairly resistant to Dutch elm disease.

A little further along the path is the most famous Japanese introduction of them all, and one of the most distinctive trees in the world. It is tall and slender with limbs that sometimes branch off sharply, even at right angles; short spurs on its twigs that look sharp as zippers or multiple stitches against the sunset; and a drooping lead shoot. It looks like an elongated pear tree. This is the *Gingko biloba*, a unique tree, more properly categorised as a conifer than a deciduous tree, but really like nothing else living. As much a creature as a plant, its females are fertilised by mobile sperm from the male pollen which swim to the ovary, a characteristic of very primitive, very ancient ferns.

In summer its ancestry also shows in its unique fan-shaped, twin-lobed leaves, which turn a glowing gold in autumn before dropping suddenly. (We also know the gingko as the maidenhair tree because the leaves were thought to resemble the hairstyle of Oriental girls. Sumo wrestlers still wear their hair in the *o-icho* style – a big gingko shape that denotes status.)

The gingko may have been around for 250 million years. It was brought to Europe from Japan in the eighteenth century, but is thought to have come originally from China where there is a tree claimed to be 3,500 years old. In wet and cold conditions it can linger as a large shrub but it generally does well in Britain. At Kew there is a gingko 250 years old and more than 80 foot high. The gingko has numerous strategies for survival. Old trees may lose their main trunks and regenerate by shooting from the bottom. It responds to stress by putting out low branches that root in the ground, making it easy to propagate by "layering".

The strength of the gingko is more than just physical. There is something downright weird in its genetic composition that enables it to resist the worst horrors man has devised. Several gingkos survived the atomic bomb dropped on Hiroshima in 1945. One of these was in the Housenbou temple, not a mile from the centre of the blast. The temple was utterly destroyed, and in 1994 a new temple was built around the still-living tree.

The gingko gives hope, but in its composed, discreet way it is also a terrifying tree. You are looking both at evidence for the indestructibility of the natural life force and confirmation that humans are poorly equipped in comparison with a plant. The longevity of the ginkgo has led it to be revered in Japan and China much as the yew is in Britain. It also contributes significantly to the natural medicine chest. Extracts from the leaves are used to treat circulatory problems and dementia. Ten years ago the trade in gingko products was worth $100 million a year in North America alone. Most of the raw product was supplied by a single farm in South Carolina which has about ten million gingkos.

It also is a stinker. The fruits of the female are small plums that have a strong fecal smell when ripe and may cause dermatitis. (Tree surgeons tell me that they have been kicked out of pubs when they have been working on gingkos and have come into contact with the fruit.) Inside the flesh are small nuts, mildly toxic to some people, considered sweet, tasty delicacies in the Far East and used for treating everything from asthma to impotence.

In the West our admiration for the gingko is tempered by our distaste for the fruit, so we prefer to plant non-fruiting male trees and guarantee the sex by cuttings or grafts. (One of the clones now frequently planted is the particularly upright sentry gingko.) As was the case with other species of tree, from apples to elms, this limits the genetic base and increases the possibility that the gingko may become vulnerable to disease.

Like the foxglove, the gingko is now edging out of the park and garden and into our streets in anticipation of drier, warmer times to come. Its roots are no problem and it does not spread massively. A street of gingkos would make a fine sight in the autumn and would be infinitely more interesting than limes. But they would have to be exclusively males, and therefore genetically vulnerable. We may be doing what time and the bomb could not: we may love the gingko to death.

The night is falling and we can hear the park-keeper scraping chains through the hasps on the park gates. We have a last stop to make in America, so let us hop back into the boat and negotiate one last bend in the dark river, to where the tulip tree, the catalpa and the sweet gum are now sunk in darkness.

The tulip tree was brought to Britain from America in the early seventeenth century, possibly by the Tradescants of London, and has been a much-loved but misunderstood feature of private gardens since. Clearly, few of the people who buy it can have read the label, because all too often it is stuffed into borders, apparently in the expectation that it will be a tree the size of a crab apple. True, it is a gorgeous tree, but huge with it. In this park, the mature tulip tree has grown into a shaggy chimney 100 foot high.

The flowers, intricate cups containing a mixture of pale

green, orange and yellow, sometimes do not appear until the tree is 20 years old. Its bark is green-brown and corky, patterned as if by beetle tracks. By far the most distinctive feature of the tree at any age is its foliage, which is a more than adequate apology for the long wait for flowers: the leaves are big and four-lobed, shaped like stumpy mittens or a child's imperfect attempts at cut-out hands. Or, if you can remember them, the Space Invaders. The autumn colour is a brilliant liquid gold.

We might think it sacrilegious to use something so pretty and benign for industry, but to the early Americans this was one of the most important timber trees, and huge inroads were quickly made into the continent's supplies, particularly in the Appalachians. It was called poplar or popple, or sometimes canoewood, because of its use in boat-making. Houses were built from it too. Some old trees were big enough for houses themselves. In the seventeenth century, John Lawson, surveyor-general of North Carolina reported a huge tulip tree "wherein a lusty man had his bed and his household furniture and lived in it till his labour got him a more fashionable mansion."

Below this tulip tree, a spreading shape writhes in the shadows like several entwined serpents streaming with water. This is no monster erupting from our river, but the twisted form of the catalpa, an Indian bean tree, which holds onto its strings of long, thin, broad-bean-like seed pods all winter. The catalpa was brought out of the wild in the early eighteenth century by Mark Catesby, an English naturalist who is said to have discovered it among the lands of the Cherokee Indians and introduced it to the American settlers. In Britain, it only grows to any size in the shelter of cities, where it has a stark, fossilised beauty, exaggerated by its dark, cracked bark. It looks dead much of the year and generally leafs up as late as June: the spectacular leaves are a foot long and heart-shaped.

Like the tulip tree, the catalpa can now occasionally be seen on our streets, though without room to writhe it tends to make an unsatisfactory street feature, unless there is some logic in planting trees that look dead so that no-one will kill them.

More common as an urban warrior than either of these two is the sweet gum, which in the south of England I have seen planted in rows along streets that were formerly occupied by limes or planes. Not so long ago it was said that this tree could only be planted in warm areas, that it was a swamp tree of the warm southern states of the USA, and had to be treated with care, so its rapid spread is a sure sign that someone, somewhere thinks the climate is changing.

If grown in the right protected garden, on the right sort of acid soil and in the right, crisp autumn weather, it produces ravishing red colours. But if things don't click for the tree it is a like a lethargic species of teenager, late out of bed with nothing much to say for itself. In winter it looks rather like a tall, conical maple, with the same opposite twigs. Like the London plane it has dangling spiked balls of fruit, but they hang singly, not in bunches, and are like many-faceted stars. The leaves too, evoke stars – think of one of those Christmas cards, showing the star of Bethlehem and then take away the bottom ray, so that it is five-pointed, not six. Alternatively, think of a cannabis leaf.

There are many other trees we could look at: the Persian ironwoods, the wingnut, the golden rain tree and countless Japanese maples. All are beautiful and many are not so smelly as some of those we have encountered. We will have to save them for another time or perhaps you will feel able to go and play the plant hunter yourself, now that you see it is not a hard business.

The last of the light has gone and the park-keeper is rattling his keys at the far gate, anxious to lock up. I have enjoyed this no end, but I should be off too. Your home is just a few yards away. After the travel, the interminable sea-voyages, the Indians, bandits, rivers and atomic bombs, not to mention the walk in the woods, a longing may take you for some souvenir to bring home. What is there among all these Chinese and Japanese and American trees that you could slip in your pocket? There is nothing obvious to hand: they are wonderful trees, but physically remote.

Just inside the gate where the park-keeper waits, you see laying in the path some conkers, bursting from their spiky casing. A glossy conker is like an irresistible gem-stone. Put conkers in your pocket and you will always feel as if you have returned with treasure and you will never grow old. You could harden them in the airing cupboard or even put them in a pot and plant them…

Enough. Why not go inside and light a fire?

Bare essentials

TREE OF HEAVEN — Skulking suckering stinker, a rejected radiation-exposed **mutant plant-pot out for revenge**. Long fronds of ash-like leaves grisly pink in spring. Wood may look like bamboo. Favours nasty places.

KEAKI — Branches like an upraised, spread palm. **Bark dark brown and rough like the hide of a cow**. Tree a uniform burned orange in autumn.

FOXGLOVE TREE — Pale brown bark and dried seed pods looking like almond shells or gaping clams in winter. Spires of lilac flowers in spring. Sometimes a shrub with immense leaves.

DOVE OR GHOST TREE — Orange-brown bark and hanging round fruits in winter. Sometimes a clean stem beneath the canopy. Jiggling pale, ghostly bracts party in the spring.

GINGKO – An elongated pear in winter. Very upright with short spurs on twigs giving it a zipper-like look. Drooping lead shoots. Unique fan-shaped leaves, blazing gold in the autumn and falling suddenly. Offensive plums.

TULIP TREE – Green-brown bark patterned as if by beetles. Flat buds on its twigs, like squashed bugs. Leaves shaped like bats or mittens. Flowers green and red "tulips".

CATALPA – Naked much of year. Overlarge fossilised **Kenwood Chef blending attachment**, with limbs coming out like whirling blades. Ash black wood and streams of long bean pods. Big lily-pad-shaped leaves.

SWEET GUM – Dangling, star-shaped seed balls in winter. **Imperfect star-shaped leaves.** Under perfect conditions it has brilliant reds in autumn.

Revision quiz V

1. **The tree of heaven secretes**
a) Essential oils used for treating dementia
b) Allelopathic phytotoxins
c) A heavenly scent when its leaves are crushed

2. **What gives the dove tree its name?**
a) Its flapping petals
b) Its flapping bracts
c) Its popularity with birds

3. **Open almond-shaped seed pods in winter can indicate**
a) An almond tree
b) A foxglove tree
c) A tree of heaven

4. **Which of these describes a keaki**
a) It has outstanding autumn colours of uniform burned amber or orange.
b) It has outstanding huge leaves prized by gardeners
c) It has outstandingly smelly fruit

5. **In winter the gingko may look like**
a) An elongated pear
b) A conifer
c) A sumo wrestler

6. **The dove tree was first propagated in the West by**
a) Ernest Wilson
b) Ernest Blofeld
c) Maurice de Vilmorin

7. **The tulip tree**
a) Is ideal for a small garden
b) Has four-lobed leaves.
c) Has pink seed pods in the autumn

8. **The gingko can survive**

a) An evening in Peckham

b) Circulatory problems

c) Atomic fall-out

9. **A member of which religious order first discovered the dove tree?**

a) The Jesuits

b) The Methodists

c) The Lazarists

10. **A low, serpentine tree with thick black limbs and clutches of long dried pods might be**

a) A black locust

b) A foxglove tree

c) An Indian bean tree.

11. Chuck It on the Fire

A wood fire is the main attraction in a family home. It is pleasant to simply sit and stare at the moving form of the flames, and television consumption will drop dramatically in a family home that has a real wood fire. Coal is never the same. Red and yellow wood flames are better company than the muted gaseous blue and orange of coal, though coal will always make the hottest fires. Wood is also more conversational: it mutters and cackles, hisses, spits and wheezes. It has a multitude of characters and moods while coal has just two – wet and unenthusiastic or dry and businesslike.

Sadly, open fires of wood or coal are inefficient and 70% of the heat will go up the chimney. However, with a wood or solid fuel burner installed in your fireplace, 70% of the heat will stay in the house. Less fuel is required, less carbon dioxide is released, less wood has to be carried and hardly any ash is produced. Wood burners were formerly sneered at by fire snobs. If you bought a period house and installed a wood burner, you clearly had pretensions beyond your means and could not afford the staff to run the house properly. Admittedly, the range of wood burners was limited and ugly. These days the choice and aesthetics have improved greatly and an Aga or Jøtul woodburner is a most acceptable addition to the sittingroom of an old rectory.

The new wood burners are ferociously efficient. Even the smallest on the market pumps out five kilowatts of heat, enough to warm a couple of rooms, heat a tank of water and fry your eggs. If you still long for the sight of naked flames, you can remove the glass doors, though from some models this will create a 15% drop in efficiency.

A wood burner is also much easier to start than an open fire and is perfect for those occasions when it is just you and the dog and you would not otherwise be bothered to light a fire but would turn up the heating instead. Nor do wood burners smoke, while at some point every open fireplace will refuse to draw because the wind is coming from the wrong quarter or you have several generations of jackdaws' nests up the chimney, or there is an insufficient through-draught.

One all-too-common reason for a smoking fireplace is an incorrect ratio between the size of the fire opening and the flue. This should be in the region of 7:1. When old houses are refurbished and the chimneys lined with thermal concrete, the flue is often narrowed considerably and a smaller fireplace will have to be inserted. Instead, the owners of the refurbished house ignore all advice and insist on installing a large reclaimed fireback, with a massive Victorian overmantle and cast-iron grate that they have been hoarding. The vast fireplace looks fantastic but it requires a large flue that they no longer have. After a few days of experiment they are half choked to death and are reaching for the woodburner catalogue, all much to the amusement of the builders. I write here from experience. Fires that smoke can be fatal. If you have any doubts about the efficiency of a fireplace or a flue you should consult a chimney engineer.

Any wood will burn, just as any wine will get you drunk, and sometimes there is nothing much on the table to choose from. There is a lot of hearsay and olde lore about what does and does not make firewood, and several ancient ditties which I will make a point of omitting. In theory, many woods have a very similar energy output when they have been properly dried out or seasoned. Beech and oak put out 6.3 giga-joules of heat per cubic metre and sycamore and elm 5.5 giga-joules. This would make a significant difference for a powerplant but in the context of a domestic fire, it probably entails one extra languid stretch to the log basket of an evening. However, the basic calorific content is one of several factors to be considered when assessing the suitability of firewood. We also need to know if it burns fast or slow, if it spits sparks, long it takes to season and how difficult it is to cut. Some woods are all but odourless when they burn and others give off delightful scents.

Seasoning is an essential process during which the water content in the wood is reduced to useable proportions. When felled, trees might have a water content of 50%, though this is much higher in some species. The objective is to reduce this to around 20-25%. Ideally this is a three stage procedure. Wood should be cut in the winter and left outside until the next autumn so that it can be dried out by the sun and the air. The wood should then be moved under cover and stacked to permit the air to circulate freely. Small quantities of wood can then be brought inside the house to dry further before use.

All wood benefits from longer seasoning and for some wet, sap-rich woods like beech or sycamore two years are essential. Don't buy logs unless the merchant can tell you what they are and how long they have been seasoned. If you cut your own logs, remember that some kinds of wood become much harder when seasoned and you are liable to damage yourself when you try to chop them. It is generally best to cut all your wood to log size as soon after felling as possible.

Some of our most common trees – **larch, lime, poplar, alder, horse chestnut, willow** – are not reckoned to make good firewood for the home, though they may be fine for biomass in an incinerator. We like the scent of burning pine but pine logs are good only for an outside bonfire. They spit with hot resin and will leave oily deposits up a chimney. Pine cones are great natural fire-lighters. However, remember that some pine trees and their cones – such as **Monterey pine** – are fire resistant. **Spruce** and **cypress** are not worth using. **Douglas fir** is passable, but there are better uses for it. **Cedar**-wood is good and incense scented but is rare.

Each good fire wood may have its particular qualities much as trees have their characters. You can have your fire hot and bright or slow and aromatic. You can have a cheerful fire to warm a party, or a smouldering bed of ashes to stare at, late into the night.

Here is a basic menu of firewood, culled from personal observation:

Apple. A wholesome but sensuous smell of baked fruit and a gently sizzling heat. A seductive wood that works on prospective house buyers much better than the smell of ground coffee.

Ash. Contains little moisture and can even be burned green if the fire is hot enough. Though an eccentric and rakish tree, it makes the best-mannered firewood for family viewing, with a clean astringent scent. It is as if the Earl of Rochester had come back as CS Lewis.

Beech. A wet wood when cut but after thorough seasoning it makes a particularly cheerful midwinter fire with a richly musty woodland smell.

Birch. A wood for Boy Scouts, who know that it burns like petrol even when damp and is excellent for getting camp fires started. At home it is best used as kindling. The logs tend to be small. (Hazel is another small wood useful for getting fires started.)

Elm. A very wet wood that needs thorough seasoning before use. Most elm comes from victims of disease and may have been standing dead for some time, which will speed up the seasoning process. As befits coffin-wood, old elm is a hand wringer when it comes to chopping. I have found elm burns cold and blue. A wood for unwelcome guests, or the end of the affair.

Gean. A pretty pink and orange wood that splits reluctantly, spits sometimes but is still a favourite. It makes a hot fire and has a kindly sweet and leathery scent, like an old country solicitor's office where the senior partner spends most of his time polishing up his hunting boots.

Hawthorn. An underrated firewood. Slow and hot with a reassuring smell of expensive cigars and Wrights Coal Tar Soap that casts a soporific spell. A companionable wood for when you want to share the sofa. Few limbs of substance grow in hedgerows: if you do have thick hawthorn logs, split them early, as with elm. Bundles of dried hawthorn trimming make excellent kindling. Also from the hedgerow, blackthorn and wild plums burn well and tend to come in conveniently slender lengths.

Holly. Often rated as a firewood. In my experience it

is a wet wood when cut and burns too quickly when well seasoned, with a gassy blue flame. Traditional advice is to burn it green. The twigs and foliage are explosive.

Hornbeam was in the past used as an oven fuel for baking bread, and is a hot, slow wood.

Oak. The grandfather of firewoods. Others burn faster and brighter, but oak is good for the long haul, well into the night. If correctly seasoned it burns slowly with a deep, strong, red heat. The scent is kippers and bacon overlaid with single malt. One for history dons to dream to.

Rowan. I have not burned this, but have seen rowans that have long been coppiced for firewood: their calorific value is decent.

Sycamore is a wet wood when first cut. When it is dried it is at least as effective as elm and burns more brightly.

Sweet Chestnut is an irascible and potentially lethal spark-chucker, however long it is dried, though it may be useful for kindling.

Yew requires a special mention. It used to be prized for furniture and turning but these days' people are not much interested in irregular short lengths of yew. If you do have yews trimmed and do not make rustic furniture yourself, them the wood is bound to sit around and eventually make its way into the wood pile, however reluctant you are to burn it. It is a hard red wood and burns very low and slow and hot – perfect for simmering a witch's cauldron. And, though we should take the arcane with a pinch of salt, it is hard to burn yew without a sense of occasion. Yew trees are so individual that each knobbly branch or blood-red sliver seems a piece of living history. It is tempting to succumb to all those stories of the tree's vast age and think of the carbon this tree may have sucked into its bones. What – or who – are you throwing on the fire? Napoleon's breath? The last groan of Thomas à Beckett? Or Julius Caesar's gasps, as he peered lasciviously at the natives of this wet and cold island? For a moment, the fire bubbles with wraiths, as a sliver of burning wood dissolves the centuries.

Combination burning of wood is fun. Burn ash in the morning for its astringent, bright wake-up call, cherry over lunch for its cheerful spitting and smell, oak for some solid afternoon heat and to get the hot water going, and then freshen up the house with apple at tea-time. More ash is good for family viewing in the evening but if you want to change the mood after the nine o'clock watershed, then hawthorn will make the atmosphere thicker and more adult. You may think that no one would notice changes in firewood, but applewood is a smell to which even children seem sensitive. The late-night addition of yew will, of course, launch you into areas of visionary speculation and travel on the astral plane, but after all this chopping and humping of logs, you should be curled up on the sofa, out for the count.

12. Can I Save the World by Planting a Pink Cherry in My Garden?

As you set about lighting a cheerful log fire, you may perhaps consider some of the glorious trees you have looked at and wonder if burning wood is quite the right thing to do. It does not seem much of a green option. Trees are beautiful: shouldn't we be planting trees rather than burning them? And what about the carbon dioxide burning wood will generate? Is it really possible to take care of that by simply planting more trees?

You would like to do your bit and be as green and ethical as possible. We all would, of course, if we were certain where to start. This business of "carbon offsetting" and wiping away your "carbon-footprint" by schemes including tree planting is complicated, even for those who are selling us the concept. The website of one carbon offset company that plants trees introduces the principle thus: "Trees capture and store carbon while establishing once mature the amount of carbon taken in and released equalises." I'm sorry: say you could that again?

Much of the necessary science for calculating our "carbon footprint" is still evolving, but the political environment is charged with urgency on all sides, so speculative figures are bandied about as if they were proven fact. For the casual reader, matters are further complicated by differences in presentation.

If you read the United Nations's Global Environment Yearbook you will see that the average Briton emits 8.3 metric tonnes of CO_2 per annum. On the other hand, figures used by the United Kingdom Forestry Commission put the amount at a little more than three tonnes per annum. Three tonnes! That's just the global average, according to the UN. What's the problem? Aha, but the Forestry Commission is referring to three tonnes of *pure carbon*, not of carbon dioxide.

Trees do sequester carbon – that much we know. Has not Al Gore himself told us to "plant trees, lots of trees"? But the value of a tree as a carbon sink depends on type, age, location and climate, and unfortunately, there are as yet no comprehensive figures. However, it has been suggested that in the United Kingdom, one hectare (2.43 acres) of growing Forestry Commission conifers will take up around three tonnes of carbon per annum, which, as noted above, is about the same amount as is emitted by an average member of the population – if you do not include all the emissions involved in producing the imported goods we consume. To wipe out this basic national carbon output with trees, we would have to plant at least 50 million hectares (120 million acres) of Sitka spruce or something similar. This is twice the land mass of the UK. If you used a higher estimate for the average emissions of a greedy consumer, including indirect emissions made through goods manufactured elsewhere – cars from Japan, furniture from Indonesia, everything else from China – then it might take four times the land mass of the UK, planted at least 1,000 trees to the acre with conifers, to neutralise our carbon footprint.

Does that give you a picture? Well, what if we planted something else? Not just those mouldy old conifers, but attractive trees that would bring a smile to the face of passers by. What if we took our love of pink to its logical conclusion and planted Japanese cherries as carbon sinks? Wouldn't it be lovely to save the world with blossom! How many of our much-loved old friend the deep-pink Kanzan would I have to plant to compensate for my annual carbon useage?

There are no available figures covering such whimsical science, but I can do what everybody else does and make some up. For a start, the lovely pink cherries would be wholly inefficient. At 25 years old, a conifer can fix say 6kg (13lb) of carbon per annum, but a pink cherry would only manage a fraction of that. They don't grow. A tenth, perhaps – I'm guessing here, but no one else knows any better.

If it takes one hectare of conifers to fix three tonnes of pure carbon, I reckon it would take at least 10 hectares of youthful Kanzan cherries to do the same. If I took into account all those indirect emissions incurred when buying Chinese-manufactured Christmas presents for my children, I would have to double that to 20 hectares or 50 acres, near as makes no difference. It gets worse. I could not plant flowering cherries 1,000 to the acre like conifers: 500 to the acre sounds about right, so I would have to double my acreage of cherries to 100 acres, containing 50,000 Japanese flowering cherries. Wow. Just think of all that pink blossom! More pink! It's almost worth it.

I suspect my figures, though no worse than many of the available estimates for carbon sequestration, are rubbish, though they are unlikely to be too generous. I have at any rate come up with a great living-art project. The "pink sink" would be noticeable from space as a great scream for help, for one month in the year anyway. A flowering cherry is, alas, of negligible environmental consequence, and the same could be said about many of the pretty trees we love.

You see the problem with tree planting? It takes a lot of trees to deal with a year's worth of exhausting trips to the supermarket and bags full of plastic tat. And that is not the end of it. It takes carbon resources to propagate those trees, to transport them and plant them and look after them. So tree planting is not in itself a way to deal with carbon emissions. Moreover, though most tree-planting schemes are run by scrupulous, ethical people, we must still be careful. In Africa, some offsetting schemes courted controversy by funding the planting of fast-growing Eucalyptus trees that are notoriously thirsty competitors for scarce water resources.

By themselves, trees may be are unable to cope with absorbing our carbon but we would struggle to survive without them. Trees account for a good chunk of the vegetable matter that produces nearly half of the oxygen released into the atmosphere. So we need them to help us breath. Trees also have enormous practical value in many cultures for fuel, food and shelter. They fight erosion and mitigate the effects of extreme climate. In some countries, whole regional economies are based around crops of fruit, seeds, foliage and bark. Agro-forestry– combining agriculture with tree-growing to fix frail soils – is an age-old method that is making a successful return even in some areas of the African Sahel.

Our existing forests are valuable beyond price as stores of the ancient carbon legacy. According to the UN – admittedly a substantial qualification – forests currently store about 50% more carbon than is currently floating around in the atmosphere. So it would be a very serious matter if they were destroyed on a grand scale, yet this is happening

It is not bad news everywhere, just where it really counts. In the northern hemisphere, forests are expanding, but in the south the trees are retreating as rainforests are removed to make way for agriculture. In the process, the CO_2 is released from thousands of years' worth of biomass – not just trees, but vegetation and soil. Even if the trees' carbon continues to be locked up in illegally exported garden furniture, some 40% of the CO_2 will go into the atmosphere, along with huge quantities of methane that escape when the earth is ripped up.

Methane is a greenhouse gas at least 20 times more potent than CO_2. It is basically the stuff of farts. It is true that even living trees do let out the odd fart. But the vast majority of methane is released by decomposing vegetable matter (of which trees form only a tiny amount) and by farting ruminants, principally beef cattle, which in South America are often moved onto land that was formerly forested. Hence deforestation is doubly damaging – in the CO_2 and methane released from the wood and disturbed old vegetation, and the millions of tonnes of cow farts that follow.

It is impossible to compensate by planting more trees in the northern hemisphere, because those in the south grow bigger many times faster and gobble up the carbon. The most effective way to use the world's forestry resources to help stabilise our climate would be to pay the locals whatever they require to conserve and manage the southern hemisphere forests and use those in the north for fuel and raw materials.

Consumers should also be hard-headed about eco-frauds that play upon our feeling for trees. The push to use more bio-fuels in our cars has led to a surge in the planting of palm oil trees in the southern hemisphere: this sounds like a good idea but these species-poor monoculture plantations are often carved out of virgin forest. It is not necessarily green to drive green. It would be truly green not to have to drive at all.

Everyone goes to great lengths to argue that green economics work and that the lights need not be dimmed. It would be heresy to suggest otherwise. Even the eco-minded mayor of London, Ken Livingstone, wrote in the introduction to his Sustainable Development Committee's report that: "sustainable development… is about securing economic, social and environmental benefits at the same time and prioritizing this win-win approach." Sceptics must chose between the grinners and the grim: those who want to hear the good news, and those like Professor James Lovelock who think that in 50 years Siberia will be a decent place to holiday and Canada the only place to live.

The undeniable certainties are that energy conservation is more effective than carbon sequestration and rainforest conservation is more effective than planting new trees. In the short term, the only truly sustainable solution is to make what is available go further, which is not really a win-win situation, but more of a grim-grin. It needn't be too ghastly. We have to turn down the thermostat, turn off the lights and huddle together in front of our wood fire.

And yes, it is okay to burn British trees as an alternative to using oil or gas. Mature trees eventually stop growing and cease being carbon sinks and can be chopped down to make way for new trees, or coppiced as they were once before. Ideally, we can then take the wood and use it as a raw building material so that we lock up the carbon in it for hundreds of years. We should build houses from wood – huge amounts of CO_2 come from the manufacture of cement and bricks. If we cannot use the wood – and there is always wood that is practically useless – we can burn it. This is not a zero-carbon option, but it is at least a renewable resource. The carbon has already been absorbed from the atmosphere and can be reabsorbed – even by the same tree that has been cut down if it is coppiced and allowed to shoot again.

There will always be a large degree of inefficiency in the cycle, but boilers and fires have improved and more trees can always be planted to compensate. Individual trees may have a minimal impact as carbon sinks, but if wood is used on a large scale as an alternative to gas or oil in heating, then the benefit expands greatly. The very process of burning wood encourages energy conservation. If you cut your own logs it sets you thinking about how much heating you need and you'll probably be too sweaty to sit bythe hearth.

So chuck another log on the fire – provided the fire is an efficient one – and feel better for it, especially if you are looking at the flames through the dim gloaming of an energy conscious home. If you have a wood burner you might have the kettle singing on top of it while it also heats the bathwater. I know it is hard to look at an ash or an oak and see it as planks and logs, much as it is hard to look at a friendly sheep and see chops. Many of us have a bit of the tree vegetarian in us and want trees to be our friends, but we must in this case, strive to be omnivorous.

Alder

Hawthorn

Oak

Lime

Beech

Pear

Horse Chestnut

Ash

Tulip

Gingko

Tree sniffs

TREES WITH DELIGHTFUL OR WHOLESOME SCENTS

Apples – toasted honey and almonds
Black locust – vanilla ice cream
Douglas fir – grapefruit scented foliage
Foxglove tree – strawberry pancakes
Gean – sunshine champagne
Limes – summer evening intoxication
Medlar – flowers smell of Pimms with cucumber
Pines – bath-time in the woods. Austrian Pine especially good
Walnut – crushed leaves are heaven for those with a polish fetish

TREES WITH SO-SO ODOURS.

Bird cherry – cheap sour fruit sweets from cornershop
Elder – in excess, flowers are like the dregs of a wine bottle
Gingko bilboa fruits – got something on your shoe?
Horse chestnut and sweet chestnut – bit priapic
Manna ash – sweet but sickly smell of candyfloss
Thorns – hawthorn too unwashed for some. Lavellei's thorn like cat's pee.
Tree of heaven – bottom of the dustbin. Ugh.

Interesting ornamental **trees for the garden**

These will establish themselves in moist but well-drained soil: heavy, cold clay should be removed from the planting pit and water must be provided during the tree's infancy. Some are sensitive and need shelter. All can be sourced through the Royal Horticultural Society plant finder and many have an RHS Award of Garden Merit. If planting near physical structures, particularly an old house, use the final height of the tree as a rough guide to the extent of future root growth. (The sizes given here are approximate maximums in the UK and are generally exceptional. Many of these trees will not reach maturity for 50 years or more.)

Strawberry tree – polite evergreen with lovely fake fruit. 50ft
Hybrid strawberry tree – as above, orange bark. (Have seen aphid problems in some areas). 50ft
Chilean myrtle – good bark colour on aromatic evergreen. (tends to be shrubby). 60ft
Paper-bark maple – irresistible to the obsessive scab peeler. 50ft
Silver birch "Grayswood Ghost" – freaky nudity in the shrubbery. 60ft (Don't worry. Birches are mostly short-lived.)
Chinese red birch – various versions offering more beautiful bark for exfoliant fiddlers. 60ft

Highclere holly "Camelliifolia" – elegant violet in leaves. Snob value. (Hollies can be trimmed as shrubs and grown quite close to property)

Silver hedgehog holly – ugly but compelling ancient cultivar

Perry's silver weeping holly – the odd twist to the leaves makes it a lively weeper

Black mulberry – make sure it is a good sized one. 40ft

Cherry "Shirofugen" – the spreading cloud: Japanese name means "white god". Needs a wide lawn. 30ft

Cherry "Subhirtella Autumnalis" – the winter cherry. Peerless by sheltered front door. 30ft. Oops. Shouldn't really plant it so close...

Cherry "Shotgetsu" – also known as "Shimidsu" which means something like "full moon behind a pine tree". Long flowering, dangling white, frilly ballerina's dress flowers. 20ft

Japanese apricot "Omoi-no-mama" – bit of a punt, as this small, delicate tree is tender and blossom comes very early. When the flowers do survive early spring frosts they are honey scented. And pink! Never more than a large bush

Crab apple "John Downie" – good pollinator, good flowers, yummy fruit. 30ft

Japanese crab – low and spreading. Beats most Japanese cherries for flower-power. 25ft

Siebold's crab – stooped tree with dagger-shaped leaves and glorious flowers. Follows on from above. 20ft

Himalayan pear – complex coloured flowers and excellent colour. Worth the pong. A very rare tree, currently only one for sale in the UK and I just bought it – hurrah!

Willow-leafed pear– popular, charming tree with soft grey pointed foliage. 40ft

Judas tree – the purple flowers are spectacular and shoot direct from bark. Plant it near lilac and visitors will imagine it smells as good as it looks. Can be heavily cut back. Needs sun. 40ft

Glastonbury thorn – terrify climate-obsessed friends with your spooky winter flowering hawthorn! Mystic value. 50ft

Tansy-leafed hawthorn– ornate grey leaves and big yellow fruit. 25ft

Hawthorn "Crimson Cloud" – rich pink blossom but broken by a white eye which lightens the tree. Pink! 25ft

Broad-leafed cockspur thorn – popular, exceptionally reliable garden tree that does everything except the washing up. 40ft

Alder-leafed whitebeam – discreet, strongly formed, attractive blossom and autumn colour. Snob value. 50ft

Vilmorin's rowan – has white flowers and pink-blush fruit and delicate leaves. Pink! Discovered by the same Lazarist who brought us the dove tree. 25ft. Plant with…

Kashmir rowan – has pink-blush flowers and white fruit. More pink! This pair looks especially romantic planted over naturalized pink Autumn crocuses. Somewhat sensitive to extreme weather. 25ft

Hornbeam *turczaninowii* – in winter a delightfully feathery nude. Can grow big. Snob value. 30ft

Black locust hybrid x *slavinii* **"Hillieri"** – a compact and less problematic version of our tough old street friend *Robinia pseudoacacia*. And it has pink flowers. Pink! Well, sort of. Good out front. 30ft

Japanese maple "Sango-Kaku" – the red bark tree. Like Spiderman. 30ft, but unlikely

Japanese maple *"Aconitifolium"* – fine leaves. Very fierce autumn colour. 30ft.

Bentham's cornel – a beautiful Himalayan dogwood with dangling red fruit once very tender in northern climates, may now grow better. 50ft

Medlar – more bush than tree. Cucumber-scented white flowers: fruits that need to decompose or "blet" before becoming edible. Dinner party value. (Defy guests to eat a bletted medlar)

Sources & further reading

Some of these may be out of print but can doubtless be obtained through dealers on Amazon:

Royal Horticultural Society Plantfinder (RHS & Dorling Kindersley). Those taxonomists can never stop fiddling with names. This is the essential guide to finding out what your favourite tree is called this year. Mind, you must possess this year's edition. A wizard publishing wheeze.

Collins How to identify Trees (1996) Patrick Harding & Gill Tomblin. Useful entry level guidebook with limited species and good pages on "confusables". Excellent for younger readers.

Collins Tree Guide (2004) Text Owen Johnson Illustrations David More. The best small guide. Exhaustive taxonomy, pithy descriptions and technically superb illustrations.

Collins Field Guide Trees of Britain and Northern Europe (1974 & subs) Text Alan Mitchell Illustrations Preben Dahlstrom, Ebbe Sunesen, Christine Darter. An earlier version, less detailed yet more complex in its lay-out: incomplete by comparison with Johnson and More's book but worth it for the incomparable observations of Alan Mitchell.
The Garden Tree (Seven Dials 1999) Originally written by

Alan Mitchell and published as *The Gardener's Book of Trees*, this was updated by Allen Coombes of the Hillier Arboretum. The text is pleasingly informal and largely preserves Mitchell's adventurous opinions. It does a fine job in narrowing down the field to those trees we might expect to find or use as companions.

Alan Mitchell's *Trees of Britain* (HarperCollins 1996) Yes, it's Alan again, this time out with his measuring tape, sizing up the biggest and best of our trees and always grumbling or rumbling about something.

Cassell's Trees of Britain & Northern Europe (2003) Text John White Illustrations David More. Big, expensive and worth it. Thoughtful, economic words by White (Mitchell's successor at the National Arboretum at Westonbirt) and a feast of huge, immaculate colour plates from David More. Trees never looked so delicious.

Flora Britannica (Chatto & Windus 1996) Richard Mabey. A work of obsessive love from this great nature writer, replete with profound personal knowledge and anecdotes culled from popular observation.

Trees and Woodland in the British Landscape (Phoenix 2001 & subs). First published in 1976, this book changed our perceptions of the past. Rackham proved that our forests had been worked as well as admired, and that the country-side was a vigorous pattern of economic forces.

Trees: Their Natural History (CUP 2000) Peter Thomas. A gem-like, readable and succinct book about tree biology – growth, health, strategies, structure and death. Invaluable for students and general readers.

The Tree Collector (Aurum, 2005) Ann Lindsay and Syd House. Exciting, compact account of the discoveries of David Douglas.

———————

The Forestry Commission at **www.forestry.gov.uk** has useful information on access to its numerous sites and on individual species while www.the-tree.org.uk is a fast-growing website crammed with information both practical and inspirational. There are several books about the sociological aspects of Japanese *sakura*. For an introduction visit www.humanflower.com and look up articles by Masashi Yamaguchi. (The kamikaze song, Cherry Blossom Comrades, is quoted from Resplendent (2003), the catalogue of an exhibition by the artist Lynne Yamamoto). The charity **www.treeaid.org.uk** offers an insight into the real economic and social importance of trees in the developing world. Useful information about local species and identifying fruit can be found through **www.common-ground.org.uk**. While readers may already have discovered the woods of the Woodland Trust, **www.woodland-trust.org.uk**, membership of The Royal Forestry Society **www.rfs.org.uk** offers regular visits to private woodlands and an insight into the commercial as well as conservation aspects of forestry. They also publish the excellent *Quarterly Journal of Forestry*. The Royal Horticultural Society **www.rhs.org.uk** is about trees as well as gardens and offers free expert advice.

For arboretums I recommend the National Arboretum at Westonbirt in Gloucestershire **www.forestry.gov.uk/westonbirt**, the Hillier Arboretum in Hampshire **www.hillier.hants.gov.uk** and Keele University **www.keele.ac.uk/university/arboretum**.

Latin names